2001
Hints
for Working
Mothers

Also by Gloria Gilbert Mayer

*The Middle Manager in Primary
Nursing* (with Katherine Bailey)

2001 Hints for Working Mothers

by Gloria Gilbert Mayer

QUILL

New York · 1983

Library of Congress Cataloging in Publication Data

Mayer, Gloria G.
  2001 hints for working mothers.

  Bibliography: p.
  Includes index.
  1. Home economics. 2. Mothers—Employment. 3. Mothers
—Time management. I. Title. II. Title:
Two thousand one hints for working mothers. III. Title:
Two thousand and one hints for working
mothers.
TX147.M375   1983   640'.43   83-8720
ISBN 0-688-02163-8 (pbk.)

Printed in the United States of America

3 4 5 6 7 8 9 10

BOOK DESIGN BY RICHARD ORIOLO

To *Tom, Kimmel,* and *Jeffrey, who provided an experimental laboratory for the contents of this book; and to Rose and Moe Gilbert and Elaine and Howard Mayer, who were role models and dual-working couples before it was popular.*

ACKNOWLEDGMENTS

I should like to express sincere gratitude to Heidi Dorf-meister, Cindy Albrecht, Tom Mayer, M.D., Abigail Farber, M.D., and Edward Fischer, M.D., who took the time to read parts of this manuscript and who made superb suggestions despite their very hectic personal schedules.

Marilyn Staats receives special thanks for reading and editing the entire manuscript and for giving me many, many unique ideas.

Thanks to Carol Haider who did an excellent job in typing and retyping the drafts of this manuscript.

My special gratitude goes to Forbes Polliard, Dr. Phyllis Giovannetti, and Mary Ellen McGlone for their support and encouragement while I was writing this book.

And finally I thank my teacher and friend Scott Edelstein, who was very instrumental in my writing career.

Contents

AUTHOR'S NOTE

The tips in this book are meant to be guides only and not all of them will be useful for everyone. Select ones compatible with your life-style that will result in a more productive and harmonious life. This means trying out the tips and learning through experience which ones work for you.

Sexism in language is a concern of many writers, including myself. Clarity is a concern of all writers. Unfortunately, the English language does not always lend itself to both clarity and equality. I have used "he or she" and "him or her" whenever I could without being complicated or confusing. Sometimes, however, for the sake of readability, I have referred to people in certain professions (physicians, for instance) as "he," and those in other professions (nurses and babysitters) as "she." I do not view any occupation or task as being reserved for either men or women alone, and my use of "he" and "she" does not imply such exclusivity.

—GLORIA GILBERT MAYER

2001
Hints
for Working
Mothers

1
Starting Out

GETTING ORGANIZED

Efficient people accomplish as much as they do by being highly organized. I've found that by being organized and planning my day, I have more time available both to accomplish things that must be done and to do those things I find rewarding and fun. The hints presented here will help you maximize efficiency while maintaining your own life-style.

PERSONAL ORGANIZATION

The term *organize* means to "arrange, establish, or institute." To arrange your activities to create more time to accomplish (or relax) more you must first establish priorities. Begin by making three lists:

1. The *musts* of each week and month. This list should include responsibilities of all your roles (wife, mother, employee, etc.). Don't forget your own personal needs.
2. The *shoulds* for each week and month.
3. The *would be nice*s for each week and month.

From these general lists, make up daily lists of things to do, broken down into these same categories.

Lists are useful in several ways:

1. Writing down activities makes them real and concrete.
2. Writing down activities helps you remember them.
3. Lists enable you to consider items carefully and give them their proper priorities.
4. Once you have written something down, you no longer have to keep it in your head. Simply keep your list with you and you always have available a complete rundown of the day's, week's, or month's activities.
5. It feels good to cross items off the list once they have been accomplished.

Keep your daily list with you at all times. A list is worse than useless if you cannot refer to it. Be realistic about what is genuinely a *must* or a *should*. Make up weekly lists at the very beginning of the week or (preferably) at the end of the previous week; monthly lists at the very beginning of the month or at the end of the month before; daily lists as much as a week in advance, or as late as the night before. Have the list for the next day made up before you go to sleep so that you will know how to start the following day. If you leave the list until morning, you may quickly find yourself in the midst of the day's activities, too busy to plan or sort things out yet without a schedule for the day.

I find it helpful to plan out several days at a time. This gives you some perspective on the week and enables you to spread out the load of *musts*. It also avoids the problem of being overloaded toward the end of the week. Be sure to consider the amount of time available for each specific day so that you can plan accordingly. (For example, don't plan on doing three loads of laundry on a day when you must work until five, then attend a meeting from seven until ten.) Time some of your regular activities (cooking, commuting, grocery shopping, etc.) so that you can plan for them realistically. Be sure that you have enough time available to accomplish all the activities on each of your lists. Be realistic: Do not overcommit yourself and do not plan so many things that you have to rush.

Allow some free time in your day. Things will never go precisely as you have planned. There may be surprises, interruptions, or emergencies. Some activities will take longer than expected (this will happen no matter how carefully you plan or allow for delays). Leaving some slack in your schedule will keep your day organized and in sync when the unexpected occurs and also give you room to extend or add activities if necessary. If by some miracle your day does go exactly as planned, take a well-earned break during this extra time.

Check your list periodically during the day to be sure you are accomplishing the *must do* items. Try to stick to your priorities as much as possible *(must* means *must,* and *would be nice* means *would be nice)* but do not be too rigid about following your list and your schedule. If an old friend gives you a call, it is silly (and insulting) to say, "I'm sorry, I can't talk now. I'm scheduled to look through my recipe books." In other words, do not be compulsive about completing everything on your list. If there are items left undone at the end of the day, reschedule them.

Items which might be included on lists are:

Errands, including addresses and directions

Phone calls to be made during the day. Include phone numbers so you don't have to waste time looking them up.

Household chores

Children's schedules

Spouse's schedule

Specific shopping lists

Upcoming events for which you might need to buy gifts or cards or prepare in some way (for example, by baking a cake).

Your daily list should include all essential information needed to accomplish each job. For example: "Call customer service, Sears, 374-0834, ext. 295, re $5 overcharge on bill dated 3/4/81, acct. no. 483-456-7899 ns." Get rid of items on the list that are not your responsibility by returning the responsibility to the proper person.

Review your lists weekly. How well did you do with your budgeted time? Where should there be changes? Were your time estimates realistic? Adjust future lists and planning as necessary. Keep pencil and paper with you at all times in order to write down new activities, chores, and commitments as they come up. Add them to your lists after you get home. (I carry *two* pencils, just in case one breaks or disappears.) If you don't like to write, use a small tape recorder that fits in your handbag.

If possible, use the first ten minutes of the day (or the last ten minutes of the day before) to think about and organize your day. Review your list; add or delete items. If necessary, go to bed ten

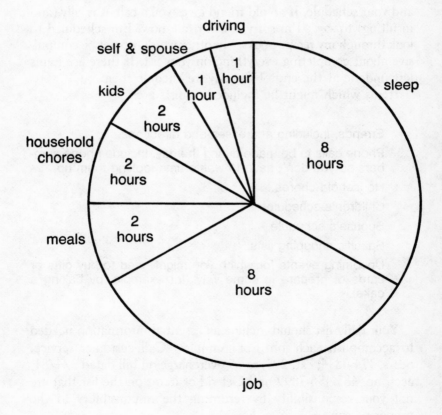

minutes later or get up ten minutes earlier to make time for this.

A useful exercise in evaluating how you spend your time is to make a pie chart with pieces representing your daily activities. After you do this, create a pie on how you would *like* your day to be and compare the two pies. Brainstorm and problem-solve (alone and with family members) on ways that the second pie can become reality. Write down plans, changes, and solutions; then do them.

FAMILY ORGANIZATIONAL HINTS

To organize your family's activities and keep everyone's schedule somewhat coordinated and in sync with those of other family members, begin with a large yearly calendar. Enter all firm dates of all persons in your family. Check the calendar frequently to avoid overcommitments; resolve conflicting commitments through family discussion. Transfer appointments, dates, and events from this master calendar to your daily, weekly, and monthly lists and to your personal and/or office calendar. Be sure to coordinate all activities through this handy vehicle.

Establish a message center in your home. This can be on the refrigerator, a bulletin board, door, etc. You do not need elaborate space or equipment. Everyone in the household should get in the habit of checking this center for messages as well as schedule changes of other family members. Everyone should use the message center to communicate schedules and daily needs, and telephone messages should be posted there. School notices, papers that need to be signed for the next day, and important mail should be left at the message center; old notices should be removed and the message center should be kept current and free from clutter.

Hold a family conference every week. Discuss and decide upon menus for the coming week. Apprise everyone of family members' schedules. Discuss and divide chores; individual preferences and abilities should be respected as much as possible. Negotiate standards of acceptability for chores (for example, do dishes have to be dried by hand or can they be left to drain?). Remember, you may have to lower standards to allow younger family members to participate in household tasks. Post a list of household assignments, schedules, and meals at the message center.

Suggest and discuss new methods and ideas, and air and discuss problems and grievances. The most efficient way to solve problems is by first defining the problem, then collecting and analyzing information related to the problem, and finally creating solutions together. Brainstorm in a family conference. Suggest as many solutions to the problem as you can think of. The more solutions you can come up with, the better the final solution will be. Defer judgment until you have had time to think about all possible solutions. Don't cling to your own suggestions and ideas but let yourself hear and appreciate the good points of other people's suggestions. Teach and expect other family members to do the same. Be sure to consider the consequences of each solution (I find it helpful to make lists of the positive and negative consequences of each). Select the one solution with the most positive and fewest negative consequences (regardless of whose solution it is); if time proves this solution ineffective, start the problem-solving process again, trying to determine what went wrong the first time around.

MAKING TIME TO DO IT ALL

Creating time where previously there was none may seem impossible since a day is only so long, but I have found that the following hints enable me to have more time than I had before.

Know yourself. What are your best times to work, to play, to relax? Equally important, when are your worst times? When do you work at peak efficiency? When are you most energetic? Least energetic? When do you concentrate best? Least? When is your mental peak? Valley? Emotional peak and valley?

If you do not know the answers to these questions, search them out. Watch yourself in action for a week or two and jot down your best and worst times. If necessary, try doing an activity at various times to see when you are best or happiest at it—and when you are worst or least happy doing it. Then adjust your work schedule to fit the best times for yourself. If you concentrate best in the early morning, plan on doing detailed or complicated work then. Deal with complex issues when you are best able to, but remember that you must allow for the schedules of the other members of your family. If your schedules clash, you (and they) will have to make compromises; this is what the weekly family conference is for.

Sometimes a compromise is simply not possible. For example, if you do your best mental work at the very time you must be getting your children ready for school, you will have to find the second best time for your thinking. Do not let this anger or disappoint you; even with the best planning and scheduling, some things are just not possible.

One great way to create time is to *hire* it. Although hired help can be costly, your time is also costly and one of your most valued possessions. You have to weigh time versus money for each activity and decide for yourself which is more valuable and which one you can afford. (See Chapter 5, page 80, "Hiring Outside Help.")

SELECTING VOLUNTEER WORK WISELY

There are many rewards associated with working for a cause or organization, and although your time may be scarce once you are employed, some volunteer work can usually be worked into your schedule. The trick here is to choose the type and amount of work carefully. Determine the causes most important to you, then carefully choose appropriate organizations and projects. Select something you sincerely want to do and in which you genuinely believe; do not simply say yes to the first person or group that asks you or tries to pressure.

Avoid overcommitting yourself. Remember that you can only do so much, no matter how much you are told you are needed, and that if you fail to fulfill your commitment, you will be held responsible, even if you were bullied into it. Decide how much time you have to give to volunteer work (an hour a week? an hour a month?). *Be realistic.* Avoid agreeing to a job too far in advance. This can lead to overload when the time comes if other pressures (responsibilities at work, for example) run high at the same time.

Volunteer only (or mostly) for tasks you enjoy doing or at least do not object to. For example, you may not mind addressing envelopes but may detest selling raffle tickets. Obtain a job description for any volunteer position involving major responsibilities. A verbal description is often sufficient but beware of descriptions that are too general and that may lead to your being saddled later with responsibilities you hadn't expected. Don't be afraid to ask for clarification of your duties, responsibilities, and decision-making power.

Feel comfortable about changing a job description before agreeing to it. For example, if a meeting is scheduled for every week, you may ask to change it to every two weeks with a telephone conference during the alternate week if needed. Find out how many meetings are involved in a project and their length and location. You don't want to spend an hour of travel time to accomplish half an hour of work. Look for hidden time commitments. If you agree to cook dinner for a church group, you may be expected to help with cleanup, too.

Sometimes you may be asked to take on additional responsibilities along the way. Feel free to say no to any or all of these; consider each one *carefully* before saying yes. Make sure all aspects of your task are made clear to you *before* you agree to undertake it. Limit the time span of your participation. Before you begin the project, clarify the limits of your commitment: "I will work on this one project an hour a week for a two-month period. If it doesn't get done in the two months, I will turn it over to another person." Consider priorities carefully. Give volunteer activities the importance they genuinely deserve—no more, no less. But look for hidden benefits of projects. For example, Girl Scouts might create extra quality time to be with your daughter on a regular basis.

Ask yourself if donating money to this cause would be more cost-effective than volunteering your time. View it in terms of your available time; driving, parking, and babysitting expenses; other commitments; available energy, etc. Learn to say *no!* You cannot continue to participate in all the volunteer activities you did before you began or went back to work. You must be selective and say no to others; they will survive without you. Saying no in advance is far preferable to saying yes and failing to fulfill your commitment later—or saying yes and becoming frantic over your many obligations. If you simply cannot volunteer for something (or anything at all), *don't.*

HOUSEHOLD TIME-SAVERS

Three items can either drive you crazy or assist you in creating more time: the telephone, the mail, and errands. Here are a few hints that have helped me streamline these activities.

Taking advantage of the telephone (and not letting the telephone take advantage of you)

1. Equip each telephone in the house with a pencil and paper that are somehow attached to it and can't be removed.
2. If possible, place telephone jacks around the house so you can use the phone in any room.
3. Get long extension cords for your phones so that you can move freely when talking.
4. When possible, be doing something else useful (cooking, cleaning, etc.) while talking on the phone.
5. Use your telephone to shop, order groceries, etc. This can save a great deal of time. (See Chapter 3, page 47, "Shopping.")
6. Whenever possible, use the phone instead of making a trip. You can avoid travel and save time by using the phone to confirm appointments and travel arrangements, to check if a store has a desired item, to learn a

business's hours, etc. These calls can save you frustration and disappointment as well.

7. Learn how to cut off phone conversations without hurting people's feelings. For example, you can say, "This is a terrible time for me, may I call you back?" (Of course, do call back later.)

8. In some instances phoning may be more timesaving and effective than a letter. Phoning, even long distance, is often cheaper, too, especially when considering the value of the time used in letter-writing.

9. You may want to take the phone off the hook during family conferences, meals, or other important events that you don't want interrupted. Most phones can simply be unplugged. If you have an answering machine, use it during these times.

10. If the telephone constantly rings in the evening, take turns answering it. Rotate this privilege (or chore) among family members.

11. Use an answering service or an answering machine if you get many calls and are out a lot. (This also screens calls for you.)

Errands

1. Set aside specific times in your weekly schedule to accomplish errands. If possible, do errands when traffic is light and lines are short. I find the best time for errands is 10 A.M. to 3 P.M. on weekdays, and all day Sunday. (Of course, many shops and offices are closed on Sunday.)

2. Group errands by location, trying to accomplish several in one place or one general area.

3. Try to find a shopping center that has all or most of the stores, offices, and services you need.

4. If possible, patronize stores and offices near your home. Traveling uses up time, gas, and money.

5. If you have appointments or errands at several locations, schedule them so that you can go directly from one to the

next with a minimum of waiting in between. Consider each location so that you eliminate backtracking and do as little traveling as possible.

6. Eliminate additional trips by making back-to-back (or, if possible, simultaneous) doctor or dentist appointments for family members (or at least for all the kids).

7. Use businesses, both professional and commercial, that do not require long waits.

8. If you are faced with a long, slow line, consider moving on to another activity and coming back at another time or on another day. During rush periods (before Christmas, on Friday afternoons or Saturdays), though, you will have to endure lines wherever you go.

9. Take your weekly or monthly list with you when you go on errands. You may be able to accomplish something on that list that was unplanned. Do not deviate too far from your scheduled daily plan, however.

10. Solicit your family's help with errands. If a blouse has to be returned, leave it in clear sight of everyone. If any member of the family is going to or near that particular store, he or she can return it for you. Attach a note with directions on it (credit to charge, exchange for a larger size, etc.). Encourage other family members to put similar errands "up for grabs." If you can conveniently run an errand for your family, be willing to do so.

11. Always confirm appointments. This can save needless travel and disappointment.

12. For tips on shopping, see Chapter 3, page 47.

Mail

1. Handle mail only once. Immediately throw away anything that requires no action or that does not need to be filed.

2. Respond only to items that *require* a response. You do not have to pay for or return unsolicited merchandise.

3. Make a carbon copy of your reply on the back of the original letter. This way you have only one sheet to file

and the chances of losing or mislaying your carbon are greatly decreased.

4. Put mail to be answered in the appropriate place for your response. If it is a bill, put it on the desk near your checkbook.

5. Letters that must be written, dates that cards have to be mailed, etc., should be put on your calendar and on your lists of *musts* and *shoulds*.

6. Keep careful files so that you can quickly locate a letter or bill when you need it.

7. Junk mail that is blank on one side makes good scratch paper.

In order to use time most efficiently, avoid interruptions. When they do occur, explain that you are busy. If you can, complete what you are doing and deal with the cause of the interruption afterward. Most people are willing to wait, be called back, etc.

Keep a supply of quarters, dimes, and nickels in your car (out of view) so you don't have to wait for change at toll booths or run into a shop when you need change. If you don't have a car, you may need change for the bus, so keep a good supply in your purse.

Use multi-service banks with direct deposit of payroll checks; direct deduction of utility payments; drive-up and walk-up windows; 24-hour money machines; bill-paying by phone; and extended banking hours.

APPOINTMENTS

Use doctors, dentists, and services that respect your time. Make appointments for the first thing in the morning so that no one will be ahead of you; you will still have most of the day left when you finish. Ask to be called if the office is running more than fifteen minutes late (make sure when you make your appointment that you give both your home and work phone numbers). Before starting out for your appointment, however, check by calling the office of your doctor, dentist, hairdresser, etc., to see if they are running late. If so, come in late or change the appointment.

When you arrive for your appointment, let the receptionist know that you are a working woman and cannot wait more than fifteen minutes. Ask her to let you know if the wait will be longer. *Relax,* especially if the wait is unavoidable. If you can (or have to) take work home with you from the office, use this time to complete some of it.

MAKING IT ALL WORK

TIME ALONE

We all need some time alone to reflect, to dream, to ponder the future. This is the hardest time to find, but it is crucial nonetheless. Give yourself this time one way or another, and use it.

Schedule time alone in advance. Put it down on your calendar. Find a place to hide, your own place in the house. Your family will eventually respect your privacy there if you do not overuse it. (The bathtub is a popular place to hide.) Learn a relaxation technique and practice it. Courses in meditation, self-hypnosis, deep muscle relaxation, yoga, and biofeedback, for example, are given at local schools, YWCA's, churches, medical clinics, etc. Be sure the class is sponsored by a reliable agency and that the instructor has credible credentials. (Classes in any of these should be inexpensive; beware of high-cost instruction, especially in anything psychological or spiritual.)

Tune out once in a while and ignore the mail, telephone, newspaper, etc. This should be done as a special treat, not as a standard or frequent practice, and at a time when you won't be inconveniencing your family, of course. Perhaps take a weekend-afternoon nap. Or relax with your feet up, listening to music for ten minutes in the evening. Done regularly, this can be very calming—far more than you'd expect for ten minutes' time. Use a heating pad or vibrator to soothe those tired muscles. If possible, try to plan for some quiet time alone every day, preferably the same time each day. Even ten or fifteen minutes can make a big difference. Occasionally take a day of vacation from work and stay in bed, go shopping, go to a museum or an afternoon movie, or do something else that is just fun. I find this enormously relaxing —it's like finding an extra day.

TIME TOGETHER

Spending time with your "significant other" is crucial if you are going to make the marriage or romance work. Accomplish this, first, by scheduling "dates" in advance, breaking them only if you absolutely have to. These should be high-priority items. Take overnights together regularly (leave the kids at home, of course) and long weekends together when you can. Or pretend your house is a hotel and do no work. Lie around, have fun, relax, and just be together. (If possible, have a friend or relative take your children for the day or weekend.) If making your home into a temporary hotel isn't possible, and if going out of town is equally impossible, check into a hotel or motel a mile or two away. "Vacation" doesn't necessarily mean far away.

Be flexible. Be willing to change yourself and accept change in your spouse. Changes are an unavoidable (and necessary) part of life. Arrange compatible work schedules. This is very important; you want to see your loved one more than ten minutes a day. Take fifteen minutes to have a cocktail (or just to be alone together) before dinner. Let the children be alone in another part of the house (watching TV, playing, or doing their own thing) if they are old enough and responsible enough. Prepare a surprise bag of activities for children to rummage through and play with on weekend mornings—this may give you some extra time to relax in bed.

MAKING THE MOST OF THINGS

Try to leave job pressures at the workplace. Spend time alone regularly with each member of your family, even if it's just for a few minutes—perhaps for a walk around the block. Reward yourself regularly for completing difficult, lengthy, or unpleasant tasks, and sometimes for smaller accomplishments—or just for getting through the day. Do the same for others in your family. Listen to your inner self, especially when things are tense. Your own intuition can give you good advice more often than you think. Learn what activities (or nonactivities) relax you and which ones help you regenerate your energy. Schedule them into your day. Remember, not every moment has to be productive. By wasting time today, you may be saving time in the future.

It is okay to do some things poorly. Try to recognize "too much stress" before it becomes a major problem. Figure out the causes of the stress and potential methods of reducing it. Be willing to deal with conflict in an open, honest, and direct manner.

2
Household Management

HOUSECLEANING

When it comes to housework, a job that's not worth doing at all, is not worth doing well.

—Lois Gould
Working Mother, January 1981

Housecleaning is a never-ending job that can never be done to perfection, no matter how hard you try. Once I came to realize and accept this, my house still looked "clean," but with a lot less of my time and effort.

Establish realistic standards for housework. If you obtain assistance from family members or hired help, your standards may have to be altered; you must learn to accept your house as a little less clean and neat than you would ideally like. Determine which housecleaning tasks can be consolidated or performed together. If there are any tasks that are less than necessary, stop doing them.

Simplify the tasks that remain as much as possible. Buy proper cleaning materials and use the right tool or product for the job. Try "new improved" products; sometimes they really do work better. If they do, stick with them—until the next improvement. Expect help, and accept it graciously.

Reorganize and streamline each room in your house for easy access, use, and cleaning. Get rid of unnecessary possessions that are difficult to clean or are dust collectors. Clean as you go; pick up and eliminate clutter.

Do *major* household cleaning less often than you do presently. Then do it less often again. If you must schedule major clean-ups, however, two or three times a year should be plenty. Make sure the entire family is present to help. Assign everyone specific tasks and see that they get done. Do one major task at a time and alternate them with smaller, more pleasant jobs. Reward yourself for completing each large job.

Replace major cleaning with minor cleaning where possible. If you have to clean alone, establish the best time. Consider when the house is emptiest and quietest and when you have the most energy and enthusiasm (or least resistance)—and when your time is available, of course. If possible, clean at approximately the same time every week. When cleaning becomes a habit, it gets done more quickly and easily, and with less grumbling. Use a preestablished routine; you will get a little faster each week.

If family members are assisting you, make sure they understand the jobs and your expectations. Have them do entire tasks instead of bits and pieces. If they empty a garbage can, that job includes wiping out the bottom and inside, relining it with a new bag, and putting it back where it belongs.

Preplan how long cleaning should take and stick to that time frame. Each week, try to reduce that amount of time a little. Do not rush, however; your goal is efficiency, not anxiety. If you are running late and have to make choices about cleaning, do what is most important to you. This might mean cleaning what is most visible to others.

Carry cleaning items and utensils in a cleaning caddy. Keep a large container in a convenient place where everyone can dump toys, papers, books, and other small items that lie around in the evening. Then, every so often, clean out that container. Only clean when you have to. If your oven does not get dirty, why bother to clean it? Ask yourself what would happen if you cleaned something monthly instead of daily or weekly. If the answer is nothing, clean that item only monthly.

Buy items that are especially easy to clean such as no-wax floors, nonstick pots and pans, dishes that go right into the dishwasher, etc. More and more of these items are being marketed, and they are generally no more expensive than the old ones. Be sure to have functioning equipment and adequate supplies. When you finish using a product, check to make sure you have a sufficient supply in reserve. If not, replenish so that you never actually run out. This saves time and a lot of headaches. If something is broken, get it fixed.

Do not overclean! Be less compulsive. Remember, you can't do everything!

SHARING THE LOAD

This is good not only for you but also for your family. Insist that each family member take care of his or her own personal cleaning —pick up clothes, take care of his or her room, etc. Don't nag at anyone to assume this responsibility—simply do not do their cleaning for them. If you want (or expect) help, you must make your expectations known. Establish ground rules from the beginning. Make it clear that you expect others to stick to them, and stick to them yourself. Make sure they are realistic; if you cannot stick to them, nobody else will.

Your weekly family conference should be used to discuss and assign household chores. Clearly define all the tasks a job entails. Share unattractive and tedious chores and rotate the hard or unpleasant jobs from person to person. Assign chores according to age, ability, and people's schedules and preferences but whoever gets a chore assignment should assume full responsibility for completing it. Job assignments should be written down and posted. They should not fit traditional sex stereotypes; everyone physically able to do so should help with dishwashing, lawn mowing, etc. No one person should assume the major responsibility for all the housecleaning and related jobs but all family members should participate in cleaning and household management.

Not many people like to do housework. If your family is not willing to help, hire a domestic. If this is not possible, do only those jobs that are important to you and let the others go. For example, change only your bed; wash only your clothes. Eventually family members will assist in doing the chores.

Make sure you have small, uncomplicated jobs for small children. Even a child of four can do something to help. Usually they not only are delighted to do their part but feel left out if everyone has a job except for them. Make job assignments fun. Have a job jar and have family members pick their tasks, or make up a pack of cards with a different job on each card—then deal them out. Hang a job reminder sheet in the household's message center. This is a low-key, nonthreatening "nag." Open communication is crucial to jobs getting done well and without friction.

Sharing household jobs with other families is becoming very popular. For example, babysitting can be exchanged for ironing clothes. Lots of creative things can be done with this sort of exchange. Explore the possibilities and find other interested families. Have combined family meetings at which all the chores that have to be done in both homes are listed, then divided according to time, interest, and schedules. Evaluate the system and make changes as necessary.

Household assistance should be viewed by all family members as a positive experience, an expectation that goes along with living in the home, and an opportunity for sharing with other family members.

CHILDREN AS HELPERS

Children can assist in such chores as

> Simple laundry tasks related to their own clothes—sorting, putting away, etc.
>
> Cleaning own rooms
>
> Bed making, especially their own

Dusting
Simple cooking
Table setting
Garden work
Watering plants
Table clearing and wiping
Washing and drying dishes
Sweeping
Mopping, wiping up spills (especially their own)
Helping wash the car
Sharpening pencils
Folding laundry
Emptying garbage cans
Caring for pets, especially their own

Children enjoy the participation and sense of accomplishment and pride they feel in helping the family. If a child does not meet your standards, it may be necessary to lower them for that one job. Jobs should be appropriate for the child's age, maturity, coordination, ability, and desire. Directions should be clear and decisive and appropriate, safe equipment should be provided to accomplish the task. Obtain miniature household tools for young children such as a small broom and mop.

If a child chooses his or her own job during a family conference, the motivation to accomplish it may be greater. Upon completion, the child should be rewarded with some status and praise. Be creative in getting children to help. Use point systems, games, pay for work, bargains, rewards, etc. Be consistent with your philosophy of child rearing, and be sure to be fair and equitable. Do not show favoritism. Barter with a child who refuses to help or exchange one of your jobs for his.

Teach children cleaning techniques, but don't expect much from very young children. Always provide a safe environment in which to function. Don't be bossy; nobody likes it.

APPLIANCES

Appliances are essential to the management of a modern household. They can be great time-savers, and they make many chores much easier. Some gadgets, however, such as electric crêpe makers, egg scramblers, bun warmers, etc., are a waste of money, time, and space. Make your decision on what appliances to buy according to your personal and family needs, the time it will save, cost, energy savings and usage, frequency of use, versatility, safety (especially for children), space requirement, and ease of use by all members of the family.

Get good, sturdy, long-lasting appliances. They usually cost more to buy but wind up being cheaper in the long run. Before you buy, be sure to ask yourself whether the appliance makes less or more work. Some appliances can actually complicate your life, such as finding cupboard space for a bacon crisper.

APPLIANCES THAT SAVE TIME:

Self-cleaning oven. This is available in most name brands and may be set to clean immediately after cooking, thereby using retained heat and saving energy.

Microwave oven. This oven generates electromagnetic waves that cause atoms in the food to vibrate much faster than in conventional cooking. This friction heats the food.

Benefits:

Great time-saver

Defrosts foods quickly

Can automatically defrost and cook without your being present

Saves energy

Preserves natural flavor

Preserves natural color

Some models turn themselves off when food is done, avoiding overcooking

Can cook on paper plates, some plastics, and heat-resistant glass

Easy to clean since the inside does not get hot and spilled food does not burn

Has attachments to make cooking more efficient, such as rotating inside table, temperature probe, browning plate (browns outside of meat)

Fairly safe to use; it is difficult, if not impossible, to burn yourself with a microwave oven

Can be bought combined with a conventional stove

Problems:

Expensive

Takes up counter space (General Electric Spacesaver takes the place of a hood and therefore takes no counter room)

Microwave-cooked food is the same texture throughout. This is most noticeable with meats. You may wish to purchase a browning attachment.

Food can be very hot if left in too long. Children can burn their mouths and tongues.

Multiple items in the microwave increase the time it takes to cook. One piece of bacon takes 1 minute; 2 pieces of bacon take 2 minutes, etc.

May be too small for a large family and/or large items like turkeys, pizzas, etc.

Long-term safety of microwave leakage still not known

Freezer. Either a refrigerator with a large freezer or a separate freezer is a great time-saver, enabling you to shop in larger quantities and store large amounts of cooked foods. Therefore, you can make double and triple portions and store the leftovers for other meals. Be sure to date freezer packages and use in order of first in, first out. Frost-free, manual defrost, and automatic defrost freezers are available; buy the right size as you do not want to pay to store air.

Dishwasher. This is one of the ultimate time-savers. Buy a dishwasher with a food disposal so you don't have to rinse dishes first. Built-in and portable types are available with many features, including a sterilizing cycle, delicate cycle, rinse-and-hold cycle, and extra-strength pot-washing cycle.

Slow cooker (Crock Pot). Great for cooking while you are away, the slow cooker enables you to prepare a meal the morning or night before, then let it cook overnight or all day. You can even store food in the refrigerator in the crock and plug it in in the morning. Many models have removable crocks so they are easy to clean. Slow cookers are inexpensive (about $20), low in energy use, and can use cheaper cuts of meat because of the long cooking process.

Pressure cookers cook faster and preserve nutrients.

Toaster oven. This versatile, easy-to-use appliance does everything a toaster does and more, including defrosting, heating and reheating, and baking. Most models do not broil meats. It does not have to be preheated and does not heat up the kitchen, and it uses less energy than conventional ovens. There are many models to choose from with varying extra functions; all are small, inexpensive (about $30), and do not take up much counter space.

Food processor. This innovation combines many functions of other small appliances, including the blender, mixer, meat grinder, and chopper. It can be used for a wide assortment of cooking preparation tasks, such as dicing, chopping, slicing, juicing, pureeing, grinding, and shredding, and is extremely helpful if you make gourmet meals or cook in large quantities. Many separate attachments are available for other kitchen tasks. Most models can be put in the dishwasher for cleaning.

Bag sealer. A handy device that electrically seals boilable bags in which foods can be refrigerated, frozen, and reheated, the bag sealer eliminates dirty pots, is inexpensive, and takes up little space. Food reheated this way retains flavor.

Vacuum cleaner. Get a sturdy, quality vacuum cleaner; it will save time and money in the long run. Avoid electric brooms and other midget vacuums—they have very little suction. Get all the attachments you need as using the proper attachment makes a big difference.

Other general appliances that may be of value include:

Washing machine

Dryer

Electric can opener

Electric mixer

Automatic ice maker (option in many refrigerators)—great time-saver if you use a lot of ice

Knife sharpener

Blender

Deep fryer

GENERAL ORGANIZATIONAL TIPS

Keep things used frequently close at hand and easily accessible. Get rid of junk, clutter, and items just not used anymore. Schedule regular raids on junk. Throw out or give away everything you can—if you haven't worn a blouse in two years, you probably never will.

Garage sales are a good way to get rid of unwanted things while taking in a few dollars. However, they take a good deal of time to organize. Consider carefully whether you have the time to spare and if the expenditure of time is worth the amount of money you are likely to make. Sometimes it's simplest just to give leftover things to Goodwill or the Salvation Army.

Have coats, hats, boots, and other accessories easily accessible so children can put them on themselves. This makes them more self-sufficient and gets them out the door quicker. Use labels around the house to indicate contents of drawers and to identify clothes and other items. Children can easily get their clothes mixed up.

Keep some extra money or traveler's checks around the house for emergencies. List emergency numbers by each phone. Always keep a complete first aid kit on hand.

Keep the freezer stocked with some emergency meals or desserts. These can be used not only for your family but for unexpected guests as well. Hang a paper cup dispenser and cups in the kitchen, low enough to be reached by children. A pegboard hung in the kitchen helps organize items and will also remind you of what needs to be taken care of. This can serve as your household message center.

Whenever possible, have items delivered rather than pick them up yourself. If you can't be home during delivery times, have packages delivered to your workplace or to a neighbor's or relative's home where someone can accept and sign for them. In dealing with services (cleaners, drugstores, repair shops), explain that your working schedule conflicts with normal business hours. Neighborhood stores that don't normally deliver or pick up may do so (or make other satisfactory arrangements) to keep your business. This is a good reason to patronize smaller businesses and to establish relationships with particular merchants and salespeople.

File folders are handy organizers for keeping similar papers together, but do not put too much in one folder. Mark each folder clearly with information on its exact contents. A desk in a convenient place is very useful for storing your papers and other household information.

Serve informal meals. To cut down on dishwashing, use paper plates and paper cups if affordable and if garbage disposal is not a problem. As much as possible, feed all family members at the same time with everyone sharing cooking duties. Encourage (and teach) whoever misses a meal to fend for himself. Teach your children at a young age to make simple meals for themselves. This sometimes takes more time initially, but the eventual benefits are well worth your efforts: You save time and your children become self-reliant. Wash dishes no more than once a day. If you have a dishwasher with a rinse-and-hold cycle, you can rinse your breakfast dishes, then wash the full day's load at night. This uses less energy and less detergent.

Color-code sheets for different rooms to allow for easy recognition in selecting linens. Fold pillowcases within the sheets so they don't get misplaced. Instead of making beds, buy attractive quilts that will double as bedspreads. All you have to do is straighten the quilt and the bed is made. Or don't make beds at all—just close the bedroom doors.

Set your dryer to partially dry your clothes while you are out of the house. When you return, complete the drying cycle.

Use aluminum foil in your oven to catch drippings so that the oven won't need cleaning. Keep pencil and paper handy in every room and in your handbag. Keep a good pencil sharpener in a convenient place.

PETS

The best pets for working moms are ones that require little or no work, like fish, turtles, birds, and cats. Dogs are cute and may be man's best friend, but they take up a great deal of time and care. If you feel you must have a dog, choose a short-haired, easy-to-care-for, even-tempered dog. If it is a female, get her spayed.

If you do get that dog, have your children assume responsibility for it. Fence in your yard so you don't have to walk your dog.

3

Shopping

GIFT SHOPPING

Have a large supply of cards on hand for all occasions. Keep some (nonperishable) gifts in the closet for when birthdays or anniversaries come up and you have forgotten to buy that special gift. Suitable items might be:

Handkerchiefs
Fine wine
Fine chocolates
Brick of cheese
Gift certificates
Movie tickets
Dinner gift certificates
Records
Gourmet food
Books
Calendars
Jigsaw puzzles

If possible, have stores wrap and mail gifts directly to recipients. This eliminates wrapping and a trip to the post office. Do not spend more than you can afford.

Keep a file of gift ideas. Prepare a list of persons and gift ideas before you go shopping. This saves time wandering around stores, looking and thinking. The list should include a whole year of birthdays, anniversaries, holidays, etc. Keep sizes with you on a small note pad. For example:

	Mom	Dad	Child	Child	G'mother	G'father	Other	Other	Other
Slacks									
Blouse, shirt									
Sweater									
Skirt									
Dress									
Socks, hose									
Shoes, slippers									
PJ's, nightgown									
Robe									
Jacket									
Undershirts									
Underpants									
Gloves									
Belt									
Hat									

Make a gift-shopping trip two or three times a year and buy gifts for the next several months. Get free boxes with your purchases so that you will have them at home for wrapping and mailing as the occasions come up.

Buy unique items from craft shows and fairs. A handmade mug, for example, would be a lovely gift for almost any occasion. You may have to compromise on some gifts by not getting the exactly right thing or by spending a bit more than you wanted to. This is the problem of time vs. money again. Allow yourself a specific amount of time for gift shopping. If you use up your allotted time and still haven't found the perfect gift, reconsider something that comes close. Ask yourself, "How much difference will it really make?"

Buy general unisex gifts for children ahead of time—coloring books, felt-tip pens, and books, for example.

Places to buy unusual or special gifts include:

Museum shops

Craft shows and fairs—but beware of shlock sold as "crafts"

Art fairs

Boutique and antique fairs (these are sometimes held in shopping malls)

Auctions, including art auctions, estate sales, and benefit auctions for schools, churches, clubs, etc.

Gourmet shops

State or county fairs

Sample sales (usually advertised in the paper or on local bulletin boards)

Small specialty shops

Specialty catalogs

Gifts of services (either ones you provide yourself or those purchased from others) are unusual and are usually appreciated tremendously. Some services you might give as gifts include:

A complete massage

Housecleaning

Painting or remodeling

Gardening

Diaper service

Rug cleaning and shampooing

A meal cooked and delivered (including clean-up, if possible)

Lawn mowing
Child care
Dog walking
Car washing
Snow shoveling

Neighborhood children can be hired to do the last five of these.

Impulse buying is fine when it comes to gifts. If you see something that seems right for a friend or relative, think seriously about buying it, even if you were planning to buy something else. Hunches play an important part in selecting gifts. But do not spend more than you can afford, or significantly more than you had originally planned to spend, unless the gift or situation clearly warrants it.

Remember to place birthdays, anniversaries, and other important dates requiring cards or gifts on your calendar and on your daily and weekly schedules. Be sure to think ahead: schedule gift shopping and mailing well before the occasion. It does you no good to remember your brother's birthday the day before if he lives two thousand miles away.

MAIL-ORDER SHOPPING

If you are unfamiliar with a mail-order company, investigate to make sure it is legitimate. Good places to begin are the Better Business Bureau and the Chamber of Commerce of the city or town where the company is based. Be wary of mail order companies that only list a post office box number.

Note the company's policy on returns; if they don't accept returns, don't order from them. Look at delivery dates. If it's close to a holiday, look for guaranteed delivery dates. If they don't guarantee delivery on or before a certain date, don't order. If it's close to a date for which you need an item, think again before ordering by mail.

Keep a record of each order. including the following information: name of item, color, size; company's name, address, phone number; date of order; and any special instructions. Keep all such records together in a convenient, easily accessible place. If you send a gift straight from the company to the recipient, double-check to make sure it was delivered in satisfactory condition. If an item arrives broken, complain immediately *in writing*. Include complete details about the order.

If any key information is absent in the ad or order blank (sizes or colors available, dimensions, etc.), be sure to specify your desires or write a query first. If you do not want a second choice or substitute should the item be out of stock, say so. If you do not want an item if it must be back-ordered, say so as well. Specify whether you wish a refund or credit.

Make a few calls to see if you can obtain the same item locally. Frequently you can.

Print all information clearly and accurately on order forms. Triple-check to make sure you have provided all the necessary information and have enclosed complete payment, including any taxes and shipping and handling charges. If you have paid by check, make sure you have signed and dated it. Keep a copy of all correspondence—yours *and* the company's. If you don't receive the service you desire, notify:

Mail Order Action Line
c/o Direct Mail/Marketing Associates
6 East 43rd Street
New York, NY 10017
(212) 689-4977

Benefits of mail-order shopping:

It saves time.

It is convenient.

You can pick out products in your own home at any time.

It may be cheaper

It saves gas and traveling hassles.

Most catalogs provide fairly complete descriptions and include detailed pictures.

Gifts can be sent directly from the company to the recipient.

Virtually anything is available by mail.

Problems of mail-order shopping:

Some companies may be unreliable.

There may be delays in shipping and arriving.

Sizes may not be quite the same as in a store.

You have no chance to inspect merchandise before purchase.

Pictures do not always accurately depict an item or its quality.

The same or similar item may be on sale locally for considerably less.

It takes time and money to return an unsatisfactory item.

GENERAL SHOPPING TIPS

Always keep careful records related to purchases. Using a charge card may be helpful in your record-keeping efforts. Read all guarantees, warranties, and directions thoroughly—preferably *before* making your purchase. If a warranty needs to be signed and/or mailed to the company to take effect, do so the same day you make your purchase.

Have a salesperson demonstrate all appliances and gadgetry before you buy. Verbal assurances are not sufficient; you should know from observation and experience what you are buying. Measure your space at home when considering a new appliance; then measure the appliance you are considering to be sure it fits.

Make sure you can obtain service for a new item in your home. Obtain advice and recommendations from neighbors and friends about certain brand names. Check *Consumer Reports* magazine, a good source of reliable information available at most libraries. Always shop with a list. Your list should include all information necessary to complete a purchase, such as the wattage of a light bulb, the model number of the item, the color desired, etc. Grocery lists should be broken down according to location in the store.

Try to use smaller stores that offer personalized service. Let the salespeople get to know you by name. If you become a regular customer, the store will want to keep your business and often will do special favors for you such as ordering or holding a specific item and calling you when your order comes in. A personal relationship with a salesperson is extremely helpful. For example, you might let her know when you will be in so that she may have some clothes ready for you to consider, saving you much time and hassle.

Don't buy anything you can't afford, even (in fact, *especially*) if it is on credit.

Keep a running shopping list and ask family members to add items as they run low. Keep pencil and paper handy for this.

Avoid waiting. Adjust your shopping times to avoid rush periods. Friday afternoons and evenings and Saturdays are generally the most crowded times everywhere.

Try not to visit a store more than once to make a purchase. Know the store's hours and call beforehand to see if the item you need is in. Preplan shopping trips. Decide where you are going and what you need, then stick to your plan. Shop at a convenient, large supermarket for most or all of your shopping. This saves a fair amount of time.

Many towns now have discount supermarkets, where shoppers weigh their own produce, bag their own purchases, and do other small jobs themselves, in exchange for prices that are roughly 10 percent lower than at standard stores. These markets also give additional discounts on bulk purchases. Though these stores may seem at first to be the obvious places to shop, you should weigh the money saved against the extra time you will need to spend shopping and the distance of the store from your home.

Every major city and many smaller towns have farmers' markets where fresh fruits and vegetables (and frequently other items) are available at very reasonable prices. Again, weigh the quality of the food and the money saved against the extra shopping time. Food co-ops often offer substantial savings on a wide variety of food items. Here again, however, you must do your own weighing and bagging, and many co-ops require an additional outlay of labor per month (usually about four hours). Co-ops sell many items unavailable in supermarkets (raw nuts, grains, bean curd, miso, whole foods, organic produce, etc.); however, some co-ops stock little or nothing in the way of health and household supplies, and very few stock any kind of junk food. The selection of packaged and frozen foods is often quite limited, too.

Plan your week's menu in advance and shop for the groceries all at once. Do major shopping once a month. Have items bagged together that go together in your pantry. Use the door-to-car service at the store. Consider grocery shopping by phone and having your purchases delivered. This saves a *lot* of time and may be little or no more expensive than going to the store yourself.

In many areas, you can still get milk and other dairy products delivered. By all means use this service unless it is very expensive. Look up "Dairies" in the Yellow Pages and call around to see who delivers and what the costs are. Or plan to emergency shop with another working woman. Around midweek call her and see if she needs milk, eggs, cheese, etc. The next week she can do the same for you.

Buy clothes that are easy to coordinate. Searching the stores for an unusual-color blouse to match a skirt is a big time-waster. Comparison shopping consumes quite a bit of time. Don't be guilty if you spend more for some item as you probably have saved that much or more in time. Perhaps you can have someone else shop for you—the ultimate! Try a spouse or child or hire a teenager to do it.

Go to sales in advance, if possible. Charge customers are sometimes invited a day before the general public. Use department stores that deliver.

If you call a store to complain or to have some action taken, write down the date of the call, the salesperson's name, and the action decided upon. Follow up at an appropriate time if necessary. If you cannot resolve a problem with a store, contact the Better Business Bureau.

4
Choosing Child Care

Finding an appropriate day-care center, nursery school, or babysitter is not easy, and the younger the child, the more difficult the process may be. Finding appropriate child care requires deliberate effort and a good deal of investigation and organization. But the rewards of feeling secure about your child's care, and the satisfactions of combining work and parenthood, make the effort well worth it.

IN-HOME, LIVE-OUT

The babysitter who comes to your home is one of the most common forms of child-care help. Most families use some babysitting assistance in the evening and many use sitters during the day as well. This form of child care is popular for young infants.
Benefits:

A familiar environment is maintained for the child.

Exposure to illnesses of other children is avoided.

Care for sick children is provided.

Babysitter might help with housework, cooking, or laundry. (These should not be primary responsibilities, however, nor should you expect every sitter to be willing or able to take on these additional jobs.)

You are the one who sets the ground rules.

Individual attention is provided for your children.

Flexible hours are possible.

Problems:

Such sitters are scarce, especially in cities.

It can be costly.

You must pay social security tax if the caretaker receives more than $50 a quarter.

The babysitter may not follow your routines.

A sitter may provide less stimulation than a day-care center.

The babysitter may arrive late, get sick, or not show up at all —and may not call!

Finding a sitter whose hours match yours may be difficult. (You may have to consider rearranging your work schedule.)

Preteens or teenagers in the neighborhood are usually hired for this type of assistance in nonschool hours. Sometimes a college student can be available to babysit during the day. To find a babysitter, use the techniques listed in Chapter 5, "Hiring Outside Help," page 80.

Many junior high schools and the Red Cross have short babysitting courses for new sitters. These courses review basic safety rules and principles of child care. Check references if the sitter is someone you don't know personally and is not listed with a reliable agency. Be specific about house rules including:

Smoking

Phone use

Drinking

Whether the sitter's friends may visit

Number of times they should check on children

Whether they can sleep on the couch or if they should stay awake the entire time

Food that may be eaten

Rooms they are allowed to use

Have a list of several babysitters. Finding babysitters that attend different schools is helpful since it allows you to get a babysitter during big events at a particular nearby school. There are babysitting services listed in the Yellow Pages in most major cities; however, these are usually very costly. Find out each sitter's time restrictions and regular commitments on weekdays and weekends. If possible, have a large enough pool of potential sitters so that someone is available (at least theoretically) whenever you wish to be away.

Find out the hourly charge before hiring a babysitter. Also find out if there is a minimum charge. Babysitting services usually charge a four-hour minimum. Is there an additional charge after midnight?

Sometimes one babysitter will give you the names of friends who are also interested in babysitting. Boys as well as girls baby-sit. Do not hesitate to hire responsible boys. If possible, have a new sitter come over a half hour before you leave to get acquainted.

In the case of younger sitters, you must walk or drive the sitter home if it is dark outside. This may be a problem if you are the only adult home; who would stay with the children during this time? In these instances, ask the babysitter if her parents can pick her up. If you are getting home extremely late, you may consider having the babysitter sleep over (if room is available). This should be preplanned. Sometimes a sitter must be home by a certain hour. It is important that you respect this and get the sitter home on time.

Plan some special activity for the babysitter to share with the children. This can be a new game or craft, a new storybook, etc. Leave a telephone number where you can be reached, if possible. Call if you are going to return later than you expected or if you are worried about the children. Sometimes a brief telephone call relieves all your worries and allows you to enjoy the evening.

Never leave until after the sitter has arrived and had a chance to meet the children and ask questions. Be sure to leave emergency numbers by the phone and to tell the sitter where first-aid supplies are.

Always tell children if a babysitter is coming even if the children will be asleep before the sitter arrives. Children may wake up and be frightened if you are not there.

Discuss discipline with the babysitter. Be sure she understands your specific rules regarding punishment. If the children are old enough, ask them the following day for their opinion of the sitter. You can approach this by asking the kids what they did together. This may give you clues as to how well the evening went. Evaluate this information carefully, since children may be manipulative if they think their report may keep you home.

A babysitting co-op is a community project where parents baby-sit for other families and earn points (translated into hours) of babysitting time for their own children. A secretary keeps track of the points. This usually works out well as long as you are willing to spend time sitting for other people. One of the greatest advantages of a babysitting co-op is that your children will be watched by adults who have children of their own.

Review the location of exits with the sitter before you leave so that if there is a fire or similar emergency, the sitter will be able to evacuate the house as quickly as possible. Leave explicit instructions concerning each child for the babysitter. A checklist follows that may prove useful in orienting a babysitter.

BABYSITTER'S INSTRUCTIONS

Child's name_____ Nickname _____

Parents can be reached at _____

Expected home at _____

NAPTIME

Child naps at:_____A.M._____P.M.

Length of usual nap_____ Do not wake up _____

Wake up if child sleeps longer than _____

Naptime rituals:

Bedroom:
>   Night lamp:
>   Shade or curtains:
>   Door opened or shut:
>   Dress for nap:

BEDTIME

Bedtime is at:_____P.M.

Start getting ready for bed at:_____P.M

Rituals before bedtime:

Bathing instructions:

Toothbrushing instructions:

Bedroom:
>   Night lamp:
>   Shade or curtains:
>   Door opened or shut:
>   Night clothes:

If child wakes up during the night, do the following:

TOILET

Child is/is not potty trained.

Special instructions:

FOOD

Feeding instructions:

Times:

Feed child_____Child feeds self _____

Rituals concerning food:

If child does not want to eat, do the following:

Policies on snacking:

Special instructions for playing with or entertaining child (include amount and type of TV permitted):

Special problems (include if child is taking any medications or is on a special diet):

Emergency numbers (fire and police) are by the phone.

What to do when the sitter doesn't show up:

1. Have a back-up babysitter "on call" who will come to your home (or to whom you can take your child).
2. A relative may be willing to be on call to care for your child on an emergency basis.
3. A neighbor or friend may be willing to help out once in a while.
4. Use a professional babysitting service listed in the Yellow Pages. These services are generally quite reliable but also comparatively expensive.
5. Use a "drop-off" nursery school for one-day child care. (Look in the Yellow Pages under "Child Care.") These are centers that accept children on a daily basis without prior registration. Hourly fees are charged.

IN-HOME, LIVE-IN

Finding a live-in caretaker for your child is usually difficult. Also, this care may be costly and may be available only for short periods of time. Live-in care is more popular in regions where foreign help is more readily available.

Benefits:

> The sitter is available regularly for extended periods of time.
>
> The sitter may provide general household assistance (cooking, cleaning, shopping, etc.) along with child care.
>
> The sitter knows and can maintain the family's routine throughout the day.
>
> The sitter provides evening as well as daytime care.
>
> Parents have more time to observe and evaluate the quality of the care.
>
> The sitter has the opportunity to establish a strong, supportive relationship with your child.

Problems:

> There will be some loss of privacy.
>
> You will need an additional room or space.
>
> You must care for the sitter when she is ill.
>
> Live-in sitters are difficult to find.
>
> Such an arrangement can be costly, especially considering added food, heat, furniture, etc.
>
> There is potential for exploitation by an unscrupulous caretaker (careful interviewing and selection will help prevent this).

The live-in is not a member of your family, so be sure to keep that distance. Define personal territory (yours *and* hers) in your home. Establish regular working hours and hours off. Keep job expectations specific. Be especially clear about house rules. The caretaker will be living in your home twenty-four hours a day.

Your children should continue to participate in household chores. The live-in should be given some authority over the children in your absence. The authority should be clearly defined and understood by everyone—parents, children, and hired help.

When interviewing potential caretakers, try to learn as much as possible (without being intrusive or impolite) about the live-in's habits. What sort of hours does she keep? How often, generally, will she have visitors, and how many? You must make an especially careful reference check. This is most important.

You must confront the issue of whether to permit drinking and/or smoking by the caretaker while she is in your home. Remember that your caretaker is entitled to a life of her own. Do not make unreasonable demands of her, and as much as possible it is best to keep out of her private life. Providing her with a private entrance (if possible) should help with this.

The caretaker may not give you any notice of quitting, even if you require it.

HOW TO FIND LIVE-IN HELP

See Chapter 5, "Hiring Outside Help," page 80.

Domestic agencies found in the Yellow Pages are usually high priced and the quality of help varies widely. Au pair girls are foreign women who spend one year as live-in housekeepers and sitters in exchange for room, board, round-trip transportation, and a small salary. Check foreign newspapers for information about au pairs.

Possible problems with au pair girls:

They are usually quite young, ages sixteen to twenty.

The girls may have problems with English.

You cannot meet the girls in advance. The interview must be done over the phone because of the great distance.

The girl's major interest is usually in seeing the United States, not in your home or children.

The sitter may become lonely or homesick.

The sitter may not get along well with your children or family. If you fire her you still have to pay her transportation costs.

The arrangement is temporary, usually one year.

For summer live-in help, see Chapter 10.

GUIDELINES FOR CHOOSING A CARETAKER

See also Chapter 5, "Hiring Outside Help," page 80.

If you already know and trust the sitter, great! Skip this part.

When you speak to the sitter on the phone, explain the job briefly (responsibilities, hours, pay, etc.). Ask about her age, previous experience, time available, and transportation—does she have her own? Is there convenient bus or other transit service between her home and yours? Get references.

For a one-time or occasional sitter an interview is not necessary. An interview is *vital,* however, if you are planning to hire someone (whether full- or part-time, live-in or live-out) who will spend a substantial amount of time with your children. Arrange personal interviews only with persons who sound qualified. This saves both you and the applicant time and trouble.

Check recent references. Ask what her responsibilities were, what the ages were of the children she cared for, and why she left that particular job. Ask the earlier employer whether she would rehire the sitter; did the kids like her and look forward to her coming? Was she sometimes (or often, or ever) sick, late, or unreliable? Do not be afraid to make long-distance calls to check references. Finding a good, reliable sitter is well worth a couple of two-dollar phone calls.

INTERVIEW GUIDELINES

Role-playing an interview in advance is helpful if it's the first time. Make a list of questions you want to ask and keep it with you during the interview for reference. Allow plenty of time for the interview so that there is opportunity for discussion.

Explain the job in some detail. If there are unusual responsibilities (such as caring for a handicapped child or cooking), make these very clear. Outline job requirements and expectations, including starting and ending time, wages, hours, benefits, vacation, sick leave, and specific responsibilities.

Ask specific questions related to the sitter's expectations for the job, previous experience, and philosophy of child rearing. Ask some general questions that allow the applicant to express her own values, interests, thoughts, feelings, and ideas. Ask a few (nonthreatening) personal questions: Does she have any brothers or sisters, what are her hobbies, what are her interests in school?

Try to get to know the potential sitter as a person rather than simply as a job applicant. Allow her to get to know you as well. Allow each applicant plenty of time to answer each question. A well-considered reply will often give you more insight than one off the top of the head. In any case, the response itself is far more important than the time it takes to arrive at it.

Check on habits such as drinking and smoking. Explain your "house rules" regarding smoking, drinking, friends visiting, phone conversations, etc.

Reliability, efficiency, and experience are not the only considerations. Friendliness, intelligence, warmth, fondness for children and for the job are important. Ask how the sitter handles the breaking-in period.

Have your child present for at least part of the interview. Observe the interaction between the sitter and the child. Remember that the applicant is also interviewing you. Allow her to ask questions, and try to give her some sense of your own interests, ideas, and child-rearing philosophy. Present some hypothetical situations and ask the applicant to respond. For example, "Joey wakes up from his nap at one o'clock, screaming loudly. What will you do?"

If there are problems with a child or in the home (child throws violent tantrums, parents are not getting along, crank phone calls, whatever), inform the sitter. It is very unpleasant to hire a good sitter, only to have her quit after a week or two because the job was more difficult or stressful than she expected. Informing the sitter at the time of the interview gives her a chance to consider whether to take the job if it is offered.

Make notes on the applicant's ability and manner, either during the interview or immediately after. These will be very valuable if you have several applicants. Get your child's opinion on the applicants. Don't hesitate to have interviews with several sitters.

HIRING THE SITTER

See also Chapter 5, "Hiring Outside Help," page 80.

Make your choice carefully. Your child may be spending as much as fifty hours a week with this person. Make the best choice you can and remember that "hunches" and intuitive feelings are important.

Make a list, ranking all qualified applicants. Include phone numbers. If for any reason you need a new sitter in the future, you can contact people from the list. Call the best applicant and offer her the job. Review the job responsibilities, hours, wages, and other pertinent information. Make sure she understands and agrees to everything. If there are points of reasonable disagreement or changes that need to be made, try to work them out over the phone. It is much simpler (and avoids many problems) if all details can be worked out before the sitter begins her first day of work. When an agreement is reached, repeat it and ask for her confirmation so that there will be no misunderstandings.

If she (or any applicant) turns down the job, be sure to ask why —her answer may be helpful to you. If she does pass up the job, call the next person on the list.

After you have hired a sitter, *promptly* call each applicant you have interviewed. Thank each one for the interview and explain politely that you have chosen someone else. If there are any applicants who are qualified but who were simply not as excellent as the person you have hired, explain the situation and tell them that you may ask them to work for you in the future.

THE NEW CARETAKER

Have any sitter who will be spending large amounts of time with your child come to your home to visit and play with your child while you are present. Observe while she and your child get to know each other. Pay her regular wages for this visit, of course. Introduce the caretaker to all members of your family. Find out from the sitter what she would like to be called, both by you and by your child. Show her around the house and familiarize her with any appliances, gadgetry, or peculiarities (sticky door, unusual telephone chime, location of light switches, etc.).

Orient the caretaker to your child's needs, habits, problems, interests, and fears. The first time, leave the sitter with your child for only a few hours. Have her come in the evening if you cannot arrange for a morning or afternoon. Try to minimize disruption of your child's routine—and your own. During the period of transition to the sitter's care, try to hold off on major changes in your child's routine (toilet training, weaning from bottle or pacifier, etc.).

The first time (or first few times) have the caretaker stay a few minutes after you get home. Use this time to observe your child and the sitter together. Discuss the day with the child and the sitter together. After the sitter leaves, discuss the day with your child alone. Let your child and the sitter get used to each other gradually. Some problems may occur at first; give them time to work themselves out.

If the sitter does not provide the care you had hoped for, or if the interaction between the sitter and your child is less than satisfactory, do not hesitate to get a different sitter. However, do give the sitter adequate time to prove herself—two to three weeks, perhaps. The first few weeks are usually the most difficult for everybody. A conference after one week may be helpful in obtaining initial feelings and making adjustments.

WHEN THE CARETAKER IS A RELATIVE

If a grandmother, aunt, or other relative is available, willing, and qualified to care for your child in your home or theirs, lucky you! But remember to take special care to explain the nature of the responsibilities, the specific hours, needs, and all the components of the job. Don't ask or expect your relative to do more than she is willing or able to do. Remember, too, to show your gratitude for her kindness, and be sure to give her a day off once in a while, as caring for even the most loving child can have its difficult moments.

Be careful that you and your relative do not wind up competing for your child's affection. Though it may seem difficult, you may need (or want) to set up house rules or guidelines for child care. It is very confusing for a child to live by two sets of rules—one while you are home and another while you are at work. If your relative does not share your philosophy of child raising or is unwilling to abide by your guidelines, you may be better off hiring a caretaker outside the family. At the same time, try not to be so rigid that you wind up laying down absolute law, or that you get angry at your relative over a small matter. A small amount of friction, especially at first, is probably inevitable, but the household should not be disrupted, nor should loving relations within the family be unnecessarily strained.

Often a pair of grandparents (or other married relatives) will be willing to provide day care for a child. This is a potentially ideal arrangement for everyone—but watch for the same problems mentioned above. Sometimes a relative will be willing to care for your child part-time—perhaps one day per week or every morning. There is nothing wrong with hiring a caretaker for part of the week and having a relative provide care the rest of the time.

If possible, pay your relative for his or her child care. If the relative will not accept money, an occasional carefully chosen gift is appropriate and very well deserved.

ORGANIZED GROUP CARE

This category includes day-care centers, nursery schools, licensed babysitters (sitters who care for several children in their own homes), and other out-of-home group child care. These may be private/profit, private/nonprofit, parent-run/nonprofit, or nonprofit sponsored by church, government, or volunteer agencies.

HOW TO LOCATE GROUP CARE

1. Check Yellow Pages under nursery schools, schools—nursery, babysitting services, child care, and/or day nurseries.
2. Call your state licensing department to obtain a list of licensed centers and day-care homes in your area.
3. Ask physicians and nurses.
4. Get recommendations from working parents with small children.
5. Contact a local child-care information and referral service.
6. Go to your library and consult reference books with lists of local nursery schools.
7. Ask a representative of any formal organization dealing with children for the names of several nursery schools.
8. Call local churches and synagogues for information or referral. Many churches and synagogues have or sponsor day-care centers that are often nondenominational and open to anyone.

GUIDELINES IN SELECTING GROUP DAY CARE

It is up to you to determine which of these items are most important and select an appropriate center accordingly. These points apply to both individual homes and group centers.

Visit possible centers and take note of the following:

The center should provide safe care for children in the absence of parents. If the center or school does not meet your expectations in this regard, do not bother investigating further. This is not the right place for your child!

Is the center licensed? Each state licenses schools, day-care centers, and child-care homes according to basic standards. A license will at least guarantee minimum standards. You can obtain a copy of the standards from your local welfare department.

Check:

1. Number of children per adult. One adult to ten children is an acceptable ratio for preschoolers; there should be fewer children per adult for toddlers and infants.

2. Space for activities (how much? is there overcrowding?).

3. Toilets (are they clean? are there enough for the number of children? are they child-size or set up for a child's easy use?).

4. Kitchen facilities (are they clean? safe?). Is the physical environment safe? Are electrical outlets covered and out of children's reach? Check windows, stairs, ventilation, heat, and furniture for safety, ease of use, and appropriateness for children.

5. Does the floor plan allow for easy flow of traffic, yet prevent a child from getting lost?

6. If the center is part of a larger building, what means are used to prevent children from roaming?

7. Examine the outdoor play area. Is it safe? Are children isolated from traffic and from other children who are not part of the center? Is there adequate supervision when children are outdoors?

8. Are toys safe, nontoxic?

9. Are there provisions for various emergencies, such as fire, injury, etc.? Are there regularly scheduled fire drills?

10. Is there a nurse, or someone with first-aid training, regularly on duty? Locate the first-aid kit. Is there a place for

sick children to lie down? What is the policy on sick children?

11. Most important: Do you get a confident feeling when talking to the director and teachers? Do they seem capable of solving problems and making decisions in an emergency? As always, your intuition is important. The center or home should feel relaxed, supportive, and responsible.

The center should provide children with appropriate educational experiences. Examine the day's schedule of activities. (All licensed schools must have an activity plan.) What types of activities are there to stimulate the child? Examples are activities of daily living (tying shoes, using zippers, buttons, snaps); language skills (the alphabet, phonetics); and physical skills (dancing, games).

Does the program seem diverse, creative, and challenging? Are there field trips? How many? What kind? Where? (Ask about the previous year.) Do children do individual projects? Group projects? Is there a garden, pets, fish? Where?

What kind of supplies are available? Do they have paints, musical instruments, work sheets? Is there a television set? How is it used? How much time is devoted to watching?

Most important is the amount of play space. This should be large enough for every child to play and have fun.

Is the children's work displayed on bulletin boards? Do you notice creativity in the art projects? Are the poor projects displayed as well as the expert ones? Is the emphasis too great (or too small) on intellectual achievement? Will your child feel too much pressure to perform educationally, sacrificing other development and fun activities, or is the reverse the case, with learning neglected?

Investigate the training and education of the staff. Be specific. Do not accept the "we are all teachers" answer. For example, have the teachers had formal education and/or practical experience? What qualifications are required for the assistant teacher position? The aide position? (Welfare department standards for licensure contain valuable information regarding staff training.)

Have the teachers and aides been with the center a long time, or is turnover high? High turnover is clearly a bad sign.

The center should allow children opportunities to socialize. Check into the number and ages of children, their opportunities for group and individual work and for free play, and the type of supervision provided for all activities. What is provided for a shy or aggressive child who may have had difficulty in either a structured or nonstructured setting? Remember, young children will argue no matter how well behaved they are, and they all need adult supervision.

The center should allow children to grow and mature at their own rate in an atmosphere of love and kindness. I have observed several nursery schools in which the educational programs were superb, but where the atmosphere was harsh and cold. I would rather sacrifice some learning for the warmth of a loving teacher or caregiver. Ask these questions as you investigate.

1. Are the activities adaptable to the individual child? Do the teachers adapt themselves and their attitudes to each child, at least to a reasonable degree?

2. What happens to the child who is ahead or behind most others of his age, physically and/or intellectually?

3. How much individual attention does each child receive?

4. Do the staff people seem happy in their jobs and glad to see the children?

5. Do the staff people seem fair, direct, and honest in dealing with the children, with you, and with each other?

6. Most important, do you trust the people with whom you will be leaving your child? Your intuition plays a crucial part in making this decision.

Remember, no center or home will be perfect. But you should feel that the staff people care about your child and that they will do their best to promote your child's growth.

The center should provide children with an environment consistent with your own values. What are the center's expectations for your child's behavior? How much of the day will he or she be responding to a teacher's requests? What is the general code of behavior for children at the center?

What forms of discipline are used for the disobedient child? Are they compatible with those you use at home? A young child asked to live under two separate codes of behavior, or receiving two very different types of discipline, may become confused as to what is expected of him. Is a disobedient child routinely reported to his or her parents?

What religious or other rituals, if any, are observed? Some centers are geared primarily toward a specific group of children. For instance, some day-care centers accept primarily (but not entirely) American Indian children. If the site you pick has a special focus, be sure both you and your child are comfortable with it.

The center should maintain your child's regular schedules of sleeping and eating. I have found this area more important than I had first thought.

Does the school serve breakfast and expect all children to eat it? Many times children eat breakfast at home with their family and may only want to drink juice or milk at school. Are children forced to eat their entire lunch? If they are, and they carry their lunch, you may only want to give them what you are positive they can eat.

Can the center handle special food likes and dislikes, special diets, small eaters, big eaters, etc.? Is the food wholesome, nourishing, and tasty? Is much sugar served? Fresh fruits and vegetables? Starches?

Do children take naps? Are they required to take naps? Is there a regular naptime? What is the supervision during naptime?

HOW TO SCREEN SITES

Use the telephone to make initial contacts and obtain general information such as school hours, vacation days, cost, ages of children, and the policies regarding sick children, giving children medicine, and picking children up late. Make an appointment to meet the teachers and discuss the school.

After your intial appointment, go unannounced to observe during group time, usually around 10:00 A.M. Observe how staff members handle an unannounced guest. This may tell you a great deal! Observe through lunch and talk to teachers during naptime if possible.

Observe interactions between staff and children. Take your child with you when you visit. How does he or she get along with the teachers and other children? Chat with other parents if possible. What are their feelings about the center? What do they like most about it? What are their biggest reservations?

Do the children have a regular teacher or teachers to whom they are assigned? Usually this is a plus. Be sure to interview the director of the center as well as your child's potential teacher. Their attitudes (toward both you and your child), as well as what they have to say, will be important factors in your decision.

Cost naturally plays an important role in picking a center. They can vary dramatically from center to center; some charge on a sliding scale based on parental income. Be sure to find out the charges and how often they are to be paid (monthly, weekly, etc.). Do not automatically choose the most expensive center on the grounds that the most expensive must be the best. Only through careful observation can you truly pick the best care for your child. For low-income families, check on sliding-scale payment schedules, scholarships, or publicly funded programs. You do receive tax credit for day care.

Location of the center, although an important consideration, should not be placed above the quality of care.

MAKING THE MOST OF DAY CARE

Visit the day-care center with your child at least once before you leave him or her there for the first time. Spend at least a half hour there with him. Let him participate in activities and play with other children while you are there.

Establish a regular schedule or routine for dropping your child off and picking up. If possible, try to make these the same times every day. Relate the pick-up time to his daily activities—for example, "I'll pick you up right after naptime." Drop-off time should be integrated into the center's schedule. This can be discussed with the teacher and will assure that the child does not miss key activities. Never duck out of the door without saying good-bye.

Mother and father and older siblings should visit the center occasionally so all can speak knowledgeably about the center, your child's activities, etc.

Stories told by children may or may not be factual. Double-check on any story you may be concerned about. Allowing your child to take a favorite blanket, pillow, or stuffed animal may prove invaluable. Be sure to label the item with the child's name.

Leave an extra set of clothing at the center in case of an accident. Do not worry if items brought from home are lost, but let the teachers know. Usually they show up by the end of the season. It is almost impossible to prevent the loss of at least one glove during the winter.

Do not rush out with your child at the end of the day. Playing is his work! If he is in the middle of a game, wait until it is finished, if at all possible. This is a good time to observe activities and interactions. On the other hand, do not belabor leaving when it is genuinely time for you and your child to go. If you are going to be late picking up your child, give him or her a call at the day-care center. The call will more than make up for the break in routine and for the wait.

In general conversation with your child, refer to the teachers and children at day care by name. This assists in making the experience part of your child's everyday life. Be sure to speak to the staff if any problems arise, either with your child or with the center. Good teachers and administrators will appreciate your concern.

Explain to your child that he or she should call you in any genuine emergency. Show him where the phone is at the center, and make sure both he and the day-care staff have both your work and home numbers.

Some children can handle separation from their parents for longer periods than others. This may change for the same child in as short a time as a few days or weeks. If this is a problem at first, you may need to shorten the amount of time your child spends at day care. Work together with staff to try to resolve this problem.

HOW TO TELL IF YOUR CHILD IS IN THE RIGHT DAY-CARE SITUATION

Your child should know the names of his teachers and aides and some of the other children. You should see your child's work displayed in the classroom, especially art projects. You should be able to examine your child's work that is not displayed—for example, projects that are not completed, written papers, etc.

The teacher should know your child well when asked about him or her. You should feel free to speak with your child's teacher frequently. Your child should continue to progress in developmental skills—toilet training, social skills, personality development.

Your child should bring home samples of his classroom work (art projects, workbooks) fairly regularly and should be generally pleased with the results himself. He should speak favorably about the school experience, although when asked, "What did you do all day?" he will always answer with that famous word "Nothing," so don't expect more of an answer to this particular question.

It never hurts to visit the day-care site occasionally to assure yourself that your child is receiving the kind of care you desire. Be wary of nursery schools that:

Overemphasize education
Present a "hard sell" attitude

Have limited parental input

Resent parents visiting

Have much lower or higher rates than the rest of the community schools

Have high numbers of children, low numbers of adults

Look dirty, or overly clean

WHEN TO CHANGE

Behavior clues of children unhappy in their day-care setting:

Any persistent alteration in normal eating or sleeping habits

Increase in nightmares or waking up at night

Acting out

Withdrawal from either parents, brothers and sisters, or other children

Clinging

Chronic crying in the morning, at school, or in the evening

Unusual fear

Persistent regression in developmental skills

Feigning illness

And, of course, an unwillingness to go to day care

These behaviors should be discussed with teachers. If you see any of these signs, speak to your child. Try to find out what the trouble is. It may be something other than the care the center provides (fights with other children, chronic shyness, etc.), or it may not be a problem with day care at all. Do not despair if your child is unable (or unwilling) to explain what is wrong—this is common in young children. If there is a problem, however, visit the day-care center to see if this is where the problem lies.

If you do see a problem—either during a visit to the center or because of your child's behavior—investigate it, then try to solve it. If the problem is with the center, speak to staff members (if necessary, to the head of the center) about it. It is possible that the staff is unaware of the problem. Do not assume that staff members are aware of (and are ignoring) a problem, or that they are already doing their best to correct it.

Problems can frequently be worked out. In a good day-care center, staff members will do their best to cooperate. However, if staff people cannot or will not help, or if the problem persists despite their best efforts, it is time to change day care. However, remember that some problems may take time to correct. Give the day-care staff sufficient time to correct the situation but do not let inertia set in. This happens frequently due to the difficulty in finding alternative day-care settings. If a problem exists, do your best to correct it. Your child should not be needlessly unhappy.

Sometimes the problem may be entirely with your child—for example, he may be unusually violent or withdrawn both in and out of day care. In cases like these, changing day-care settings may do little or no good. Do not try to avoid the problem or place the blame on others; try to deal with the problem directly. There are usually counseling, testing, and evaluating services available through the local school district, free of charge.

HOW TO CHANGE DAY CARE

Follow the procedure described earlier in this chapter to find a new day-care center. Explain to the head and/or staff of your child's old center why you are changing to another setting.

Let your child know as soon as possible that a change in day-care arrangements will be made. This will give him or her time to adjust. Introduce your child to the new center and caretakers before you leave him or her there for the first time.

Assist your child in saying good-bye to his or her former caretakers and friends. You might want to bring in a special treat for all the children on the last day. If your child has made close friends at the old center, arrange for him or her to continue to see them, at least occasionally. It is valuable to allow these friend-ships to continue.

During the first week at the new center, you and your husband should plan on staying a few minutes in the morning and evening when you drop off and pick up your child to become familiar with staff and activities and to make the transition easier for the child. Be enthusiastic about the new arrangements. If you do not genu-inely feel such enthusiasm, chances are your child is once again in the wrong setting. Do not dwell on the former child-care program. Avoid making comparisons in discussions with your child and with other adults.

5

Hiring Outside Help

See Chapter 4, "Choosing Child Care," page 56, for additional information on finding, choosing, and hiring babysitters.

First, decide on a budget: How much can you afford to spend on assistance with household tasks? Don't exceed that budget.

Take inventory of all household tasks. List them in order, from the most to least dreaded. Try to hire out the most unpleasant activities first. In general, if you can reasonably afford to pay someone to handle an unpleasant task, do it.

Be specific about your needs. Give explicit directions to hired help and make your expectations clear. Orient the person you have hired to your home and the job that needs to be done. Have the appropriate tools, equipment, and products to do the job. Check your supply of products occasionally to make sure you have enough.

The first time or two, supervise the worker on the job to make sure he or she is doing it properly. Don't overwhelm the worker, however, or get in her way. Inspect the job when it is finished, and go over any instructions or details that need repeating. Once the worker has gotten the hang of the job (and once you feel she can be trusted), supervision is no longer necessary or helpful. Unnecessary and unwanted supervision can be irritating.

Do not hesitate to replace ineffective help or to change your mind if someone does not work out.

Chores for which hiring someone can create time for you are:

Housecleaning, either the entire house or special areas like floors or windows

Carpet-cleaning service

Catering for your next party

Window washing

Yard help—from the kid next door mowing your lawn to a yard maintenance service to a professional gardener, either on a regular basis or once in a while when there is major work to be done

Sewing—mending, altering, or sewing new items

Laundry, including ironing

Car washing

Cooking

Secretarial work such as addressing envelopes, typing, answering phones

Babysitting and child care

Dog walking

Plant watering

Many of these services make excellent, unusual gifts. For more information, see Chapter 3, "Gift Shopping," page 47.

Whom you can hire:

A neighbor or neighbor's children

Teenagers

Preteens to do certain jobs (perhaps walking the dog)

Self-employed domestic worker

Agency-affiliated domestic worker

Kids from job corps or similar programs

College students

Service company (lawn care, carpet cleaners, laundry, etc.)

Persons who "moonlight" in the evening

Senior citizens

HOW TO FIND HELP

If you have difficulty obtaining someone to work for you, try advertising. If you require special skills or if the job includes unusual responsibilities, be sure to say so in your notices. Place ads in neighborhood papers, Sunday papers, college papers, or special interest papers such as foreign-language papers, feminist papers, and co-op newsletters. Post notices on bulletin boards in local shops. An example of an informative posted notice is:

BABYSITTER WANTED

Loving babysitter wanted to care for self-reliant 4-year-old girl weekdays in my home. Must be reliable and drive own car. No smoking or drinking.
References required. Salary negotiable. Call Mrs. Marks after 6 P.M. 734-2108.

This notice provides more information than something that states simply, "Babysitter wanted, call 734-2108." It gives basic requirements that will screen out some of your potential callers. Tear-off phone numbers attached to your ad are helpful.

Contact church or synagogue groups. Try placing notices on bulletin boards or asking at women's meetings. Advertise in the church or synagogue newsletter.

Call senior citizen groups or centers and place notices on their bulletin boards as well. Arrange a job listing with the work/study offices of local colleges and universities and post your notice on bulletin boards in the student union and other appropriate places.

Try child-care information and referral services, state employment offices, social welfare agencies, and employment agencies specializing in domestic help. Talk to neighbors—a very efficient grapevine—and ask at meetings of neighborhood organizations, clubs, and co-ops.

When hiring teens or preteens, make sure they understand the exact time commitments of the job. Stress to them that it is essential that they be on time and that they cannot skip a day without giving you advance notice or unless they are sick. Check with their parents to make sure they approve of this commitment. You may have to hire several teens. Because of their varied daily schedules and many outside activities, it is unlikely that any one teenager will be able to make a large time commitment. Be sure to have contingency plans for sick days and other emergencies.

Points to remember in hiring outside help:

1. Obtain references.

2. Always interview potential employees.

3. Write up a job description listing exact expectations, standards, and directions. Include expectations regarding child care, cleaning, cooking, laundry, ironing, etc. List these jobs in order of priority.

4. Pay a reasonable salary. Check the rates with neighbors and with a couple of local employment agencies. Always pay promptly for work completed.

5. Decide on a method of payment—either an hourly rate or a flat rate for the job.

6. Determine when the helper will be available, then plan a regular schedule—for example, every other Saturday from 9:00 A.M. to 5:00 P.M.

7. Be sure it is clear who pays for (or provides) transportation and what kind will be used (bus, taxi, car, etc.).

8. Be very specific on details related to vacations and other benefits.

9. Before using an agency, investigate it to make sure it is a legitimate business with satisfactory employees.

10. If you hire live-in help, it is extremely important to check references and to establish exact expectations and working times. Since your helper lives with you, it is easy to think that he or she is always working.

11. Communicate honestly with household help. If there is something you do not like, let her or him know about it.

12. Always have an alternative in mind if your regular worker can't make it.

13. Do not expect a person hired for one particular job to do others. If you want him to expand his responsibilities, you must renegotiate the job.

14. Don't settle for inadequate performance. You can always find someone else.

For interviewing guidelines, see Chapter 4, page 64. These will need to be adapted to the particular job and applicants.

6

Orienting Your Child to Your Job

It is important that your child know what you and your spouse do when you are away at work. Describing your job or career to your child is a very important aspect of successfully combining motherhood and work.

Begin by explaining what the words *work, job,* and *office* mean. Bring your child to your workplace for a visit, if possible. Be sure it is only for an hour or two; a child cannot tolerate a full day, and after a point he or she may become a nuisance to co-workers.

Introduce your child to co-workers by name. Explain exactly what activities you do at work and, if possible, show your child your desk or station, any equipment that you may use, and a sample of your work product (memos, blueprints, lab reports, a newly cleaned office, whatever). Children love to touch; let your child briefly touch any equipment you use, (if it is completely safe to do so, of course, and if the equipment is not fragile). Let your child sit at your desk or station or otherwise briefly fill your shoes. Explain what the organization you work for does. If it's not too complicated, explain how your work helps the organization.

Show your child your telephone and emphasize how easy it is to reach you by phone in an emergency. Explain, "I'm only a telephone call away." State what you are called at work—for example, Mrs. Jones, Ms. Kramer, or your first name. This assists your child if he or she ever has to call you.

If you spend time in meetings, arrange to have your child sit in on the last few minutes of a meeting. The term *meeting* is unclear to many children (and to many adults) and needs to be explained. If you follow a regular work schedule, go briefly through a typical day with your child. Relate your day to his or hers—for example, "When you are having a snack at nursery school, I am typing at my desk."

If it's impossible to arrange a visit during working hours, try to arrange one after hours or on a weekend. If it's impossible for your child to visit your workplace at all, role-play your work activities at home. Pretend you are working and let your child be a co-worker. This can be fun and allows your child to get a feel for both what you do and what an adult's role is like.

Titles of jobs are sometimes difficult to remember or to associate with a particular activity. Emphasize what you *do* at work rather than what your title is. Eventually your child will associate your job title with what you are actually doing.

If you can arrange a class trip to your place of employment, great! This may be possible if you work for an airline, newspaper, or factory.

7

The Second, Third, and Nth Child

GENERAL FACTS

A second (or other additional) child creates about one-half more work and costs about half as much as baby number one. In a one-child family with two adults, one parent can be relieved of child-care responsibilities reasonably often. Two children create the situation of one parent to each child; more than two children creates even more full-time child-care responsibilities for both parents.

If your children are born less than two years apart, you will spend fewer years caring for infants. However, sibling rivalry can be more intense between children of similar ages, and it can be difficult caring for two young children at once. Having children born two to four years apart is very popular, since the siblings are close enough in age to be friends. Having children more than four years apart allows parents to spend private time with the new infant while the older children are in school and doing other things on their own. However, you will then be spending quite a few years caring for infants.

Since no one knows the right answers regarding spacing of children, decisions should be based on your own family needs, readiness for children, financial and career resources, and your own personal goals and desires.

A second pregnancy can be complicated by the first child who has his or her own needs, desires, and wants. Therefore you may not always be able to come home in the evening and lie down and rest because the child (or children) already there may have a particular need at that very moment. Do not push the first child to develop before he or she is ready, just in anticipation of the second.

Usually parents feel more secure and are more relaxed and less anxious the second time around. You can and should expect to feel this way; after all, you've already been through it all once.

Amniocentesis may be done on women thirty-five years old or over. This procedure determines if the fetus has certain genetic abnormalities—and also tells you its sex. If you know the sex of the developing fetus, you can begin referring to the child as "he" or "she" well before birth. This helps prepare siblings and others for the new arrival.

With the arrival of a new baby, your other children may regress in some developmental tasks (that is, they may begin to act younger and temporarily lose certain skills). This is something of a jealous reaction. The child is aware that he will be sharing your love and attention with another child and hopes to gain some of it back by acting more childish himself. This occurs quite frequently but if you simply ignore it, it will pass in a few weeks—as long as the child feels that he continues to have the love of his or her parents.

Be sure to find out how your new pregnancy will affect your job. For example, what are the arrangements, terms, and conditions for maternity leave, if any? Decide what changes you will need to make in your work schedule during your pregnancy or after the birth, and develop a strategy on how and when to tell your employer so as not to lose any job status or seniority. Make it clear when you will be returning to work and what hours you can or would like to work when you return.

Discuss with your husband the possibility of his taking paternity leave. Some employers now grant such leaves on a reasonably regular basis.

There are many innovative options for the delivery of the new baby:

1. Many hospitals now have birthing rooms which are far cozier and more comfortable than hospital delivery rooms.
2. The father and your other children can be present at the delivery.
3. The baby can be born at home, with the assistance of either a doctor or a midwife.
4. A birthing chair can be used for a more comfortable delivery.
5. The father can cut the umbilical cord and hold the baby immediately.
6. Shortened hospital stays—sometimes as short as twenty-four hours—are now possible.

Obviously, most of these options are available for the birth of a first baby, too. Mothers of later children, however, are usually more open to these kinds of alternatives than first-time mothers.

PREGNANCY

Once you have a child, later pregnancies become known territory. However, there are always enough differences and unknowns to make each pregnancy unique, exciting, and special. One of the main differences is that you have a child already who needs your love and attention. The exhaustion, leg swelling, and need to relax may be as present in the second pregnancy as they were in the first, but your child may require your time after work. Therefore, the luxury of coming home and napping may not be as available. The more children you have, the less time is available for yourself.

Remember, however, that you must maintain your mental and physical health for the good of yourself, the developing baby, and your whole family. Since you are already kept busy by a child and a job, you will need routines for getting essential rest. You might:

Lie in bed with your first child and read stories or review classwork with him or her. You can then get those tired legs up

Lie down and allow your child to read to you and show you pictures the way the teacher does in kindergarten

Put a TV in your bedroom so you can lie down with your child and watch a favorite show

Get a lounge chair with an ottoman so you can prop your feet up while sharing time with your family

On very busy and tiring days, have Dad take all the children out to dinner while you nap

Hire a babysitter to watch your children while you rest

If you are planning to work throughout your pregnancy, be sure to inform your physician so that the doctor can accommodate your time schedule for your regular appointments. Make it clear that if the physician has an emergency or is running significantly late on days when you have an appointment, you expect to be notified immediately.

Take a review class in childbirth preparation and infant care. You do forget many things as time passes. Begin to arrange child care for the newborn in the fourth or fifth month of pregnancy. Interview potential babysitters and discuss your needs. (See Chapter 4, "Choosing Child Care.") Do not assume your older children will babysit for you. You should decide on baby-sitting policies well before the arrival of the new infant. For the sake of convenience and simplicity, the sitter for the new baby should live near your home, your work, or your other child's school.

Make arrangements for where the other children will stay during your hospitalization. Explain to them why you are going to the hospital. If they are sleeping over at someone's house and are not used to doing this, have a trial run before the delivery date. (Neither having a hospital delivery nor having the children spend time away from home is strictly necessary, of course.)

PREPARATION OF OLDER CHILDREN

Tell your children about your pregnancy early so they have time to get used to it and to the idea of having a new brother or sister. There are several excellent books on preparing the first child for the arrival of the second. One or two of these should be read to your children.

If you want a two-year-old to give up the crib, do it long before your due date. Put the crib away and make a big fuss about the first child's new room and grown-up bed. When the new baby arrives, the crib may not even be recognized by its former occupant as his own.

There are some new-child preparation classes for young siblings. If these are offered in your community, it may be worthwhile to allow your children to participate. If none is offered, work with your local community center to get one going.

Explain to your children about pregnancy and birth so that they will have some idea what you are going through. Answer frankly and directly any questions they may have and dispel any myths or half-truths about sex, pregnancy, or birth that they may have picked up elsewhere. When you begin showing, you may want to use pictures to show your children what is happening to the fetus. There are models available to show children fetal development. Ask at your doctor's office, your hospital, or perhaps the public library.

Make it clear to the first child that you will continue to have the same relationship with him or her after the second child is born. Point out positive and negative changes that might happen after the arrival of the new baby—for example, you will be getting up in the middle of the night a lot. The more your child is aware of the changes in advance, the less upsetting they will be.

Take children with you to the doctor for your prenatal checkups and allow them to listen to the fetus's heartbeat. They are fascinated by this, and actually hearing the heart makes the whole thing more real to them. Let your children place their hands on your belly and feel the fetus move.

If possible, allow your child to watch an animal (cat, dog, cow, guinea pig) give birth. He or she can touch or play with the newborn animal. You can then explain the birth process and point out the similarities between the birth of the animal and the upcoming birth of your new baby.

During your pregnancy, institute one or two special activities with your children that can continue after the arrival of the new baby. For instance, perhaps you and the children can all have a special lunch together on Saturdays. When the new baby is born, Dad can babysit for the infant while you and the older children can spend some special time together.

Be sure to let your children's teachers and sitters know you are pregnant and tell them your due date. If your children are acting out or are feeling sad or happy, the teachers will then know the cause and be able to deal with your children more easily and effectively.

Keep up old routines and rituals with the children. If some have to be given up, do it well before the birth of the new baby so the other children won't think of it as a "sacrifice" for the new member of the family.

When choosing a hospital for your delivery, check on sibling visitation policies. Make sure your children can visit as much as you want them to. Explain to your children what will happen during your labor, delivery, and hospitalization. Do your best to answer any questions they may have. Let them know well in advance what the arrangements for their care will be while you are away.

Point out other babies to your children in grocery stores, in the park, and elsewhere. Include the children in buying the baby's clothes and furniture. Let them help in designing the baby's room. But do not overprepare them. They should be excited at the prospect of a new brother or sister, not weary of it.

Do not promise other children a particular sex for the new

baby unless you know for sure through a physician and amnio-centesis. Do not believe old wives' tales such as predicting sex by heart rate.

You may want to arrange something special for your other children while you are in the hospital. If Dad or grandparents are staying with the children, arrange a special trip. Or you might want to leave presents hidden around the house where children can find them with clues you give them over the phone. Try to make arrangements for this treat at least a month before your due date so that your children can enjoy it even if the birth is prema-ture.

Take a picture of your children to the hospital and put it up so all can see. When the children visit you, they will be very proud that they are displayed along with the newborn. Call your chil-dren from the hospital to tell them how much you love them. (Do the same for your husband, of course.) Do not talk too much about the new baby with your other children. Rather, concentrate your conversation on activities they are interested in. Give them your phone number so they can call you if they need you.

Be sure to allow children to see their new sibling as soon after the birth as possible. If the children are old enough, let them fondle or hold the baby.

BACK HOME WITH THE NEW BABY

When arriving home with the new baby, try to let someone else hold him so your arms can be free to hug and embrace the other children. Always address each child by his or her name, even when speaking about two or more at a time. Do not refer to them as "the kids." Refer to the new baby as "our baby."

Have a babysitter stay with the newborn for a while so you can spend some time alone with your other children. Take out the family photo album and allow the children to look at themselves as babies. If you are breast-feeding the new baby, show pictures of the other children breast-feeding as infants, or at least of being held and loved. Point out each child by name.

Continue to keep up routines and rituals with the other children. Give them things to eat while feeding the infant. This way they will feel equally cared for. (Don't overfeed them, of course.)

Allow your children to hold and touch the new baby. Keep the infant in view of the other children. You may wish to put a stool or chair by the crib; the children can stand on it to watch the baby. Avoid any major changes with the arrival of the new baby. This helps keep family life stable and avoids upsetting the other children.

SIBLING RIVALRY

Sibling rivalry is the competition between brothers and sisters for what they perceive as their fair share of parental approval, attention, time, toys, and love. It is common and normal and to a large degree unavoidable. Therefore, you should not look on sibling rivalry with too much disapproval. Brothers and sisters who fight can also be friends. They can and do love, support, and play with each other at other times.

Consistent behavior by parents is important in all aspects of child rearing and helps in moderating sibling rivalry. For example, if you give a reward to each child for good behavior (or administer punishment for breaking rules), there will be no chance for any child to feel you love his brother or sister more than you love him.

Always thank children for their assistance. If children feel or act hostile, encourage them to redirect their hostility to a punching bag, stuffed animals, dolls, or in competitive sports.

Children with positive self-concepts and high self-esteem have less of a need for sibling rivalry. Try to help your children develop this. Children cannot always be treated exactly equally, and both you and your children should accept that "fair" does not always mean "equal." Each child should be treated as the unique individual he or she is, and in each case the circumstances must be taken into account.

When older children are fighting, it is better to let them work it out for themselves rather than to interfere, at least as long as no one gets hurt. Do not play judge and jury in sibling fights. Instead, try to *assist* in problem-solving to arrive at a fair answer or alternative.

Do not allow older siblings to take responsibility for younger ones unless the age difference is great. The younger child probably will not accept the older one in this role, and this can cause a frustrating and dangerous situation. Do not force older children to help care for younger ones if they don't want to.

A kitchen timer is helpful in timing the sharing of toys and activities. Use distraction and redirection to avoid potential fights or to stop ongoing battles. For example, during a heated verbal argument, say, "Come quick and look at this beautiful blue jay, it's the biggest and bluest I've ever seen." Sometimes the fight will be immediately dropped and forgotten. (Don't be too obvious about using distraction, however, and don't try to use it too often. Your children will catch on quickly and the technique will no longer work.)

Teach young children the words *compromise* and *cooperate* and their meanings. Then insist on their putting these concepts into practice. This will be useful to them not only at home, but later on in life as well—at play, in school, and as adults. Do not brag about one child to the other and never compare their accomplishments, disappointments, and development. Never speak critically of a child in front of his brother or sister. Each child should receive his full share of praise and reward for his achievements. Each should also be made aware of the achievements of his brothers and sisters.

When picking up two or more kids from different places, use the time driving alone with one child to communicate on a one-to-one basis. Try to alternate whom you pick up first if possible.

BEYOND SIBLING RIVALRY: POINTS TO REMEMBER

Sibling love and loyalty are emotions that can (and almost always do) outlast sibling rivalry. If children attend the same nursery school or grade school, they usually support and care for each other and feel more secure because they are two instead of one. If there are two or more older children that have to stay home alone, they usually will keep each other company (although sometimes they do fight).

Siblings can play together and entertain each other, allowing parents some time for themselves. Tools learned by a child for getting along with a sibling—for example, cooperation and compromise—are useful in life in general.

Siblings usually stick together when negotiating for something with parents. They give each other support. Older sisters and brothers introduce new words, games, and experiences to younger siblings. Sometimes these are things that can only pass from child to child, and never from adult to child. Sibling love extends well beyond the years at home and can serve as a great source of security and strength when the children become adults.

Remember, few parents report regret that they had more than one child, even with all the extra work and problems of two or more children.

8

Sick Kids

When "M.D." or "physician" is mentioned in this chapter, other health care professionals (such as physician's assistants or nurse practitioners) can often be equally helpful.

I frequently recommend giving children acetaminophen, a nonaspirin drug that, like aspirin, relieves pain and reduces fever. It is available without a prescription in drug and variety stores under several brand names the best known of which is Tylenol.

GUARD AGAINST ILLNESS AND INJURY

The best way to avoid the problems of sick children is to prevent illness. This is an almost impossible task, however, especially when it comes to the common cold, but there are certain steps that can be taken to keep children healthy. Begin by following the recommended immunization schedule, which can be obtained from any physician's office or public health agency. Routine physical examinations also assure you of your child's normal growth and development; they are recommended at approximately the following ages:

2–3 weeks
2 months
4 months
6 months
10 months

18 months
2 years
3 years
5 years
11–12 years
15 years

Encourage healthy eating habits (see pages 175 to 176 for more information) and from ten to fourteen hours of sleep daily to allow for an active day's schedule. Regular exercise is important, too.

There are more than 200 viruses that cause the common cold. It is impossible to protect children from all of these and during the first year in school or preschool, your child may experience a continuous "cold" (it may be allergy). Children who go to a preschool will begin being exposed to these viruses at an earlier age and may develop enough immunity to save them from repeated absences in kindergarten. However, on the whole, there is little you can do to prevent this very common illness.

Children should practice mouth and teeth hygiene (brushing and flossing) twice daily. Regular annual visits to the dentist should begin at age two. Flossing is now recommended for children as young as two or three.

Safety at home is crucial. This includes the entire home environment, including garage, attic, basement, closets, and yard. Put all poisons far out of the reach of children. "Mr. Yuk" stickers, available at your local poison control center, are very effective and should be put on all poisonous materials. An accident prevention program should be actively maintained, including:

Cleaning stairways to prevent falls
Tucking electrical cords away
Covering electrical outlets
Placing decals on glass sliding doors

Using childproof caps
Putting all medicines and poisons out of reach
Cleaning up spills immediately
Using a night light
Using Mr. Yuk stickers

HYGIENE RULES FOR SICK CHILDREN

Cover your mouth and nose with a clean tissue or handkerchief when you sneeze or cough. Do not sneeze or cough in other people's faces. Throw away used tissues in the garbage can or toilet immediately, never in a wastepaper basket. Wash your hands frequently, especially after sneezing and coughing.

GENERAL HEALTH RULES

In checking whether your child has an elevated temperature, you *must* use a thermometer. Feeling the child's forehead or body is not accurate in detecting a fever. Take your child's temperature while he is healthy so you know what is normal for him: 98.6° is not everyone's normal temperature, and temperatures are often a bit higher later in the day.

Acetaminophen and aspirin are completely different drugs, although they act similarly to reduce fever and relieve pain. Recently, aspirin has been associated with the initiation of other diseases and is not prescribed as frequently as it once was. In fact, all drugs for children should be given with great discretion and as rarely as possible. In this chapter, acetaminophen will be recommended when a drug for reducing pain or fever is needed, but aspirin can be used instead or even along with acetaminophen, since they are different drugs. Check with your physician for the most current advice on giving aspirin and acetaminophen to children.

A ten-day course of medication is exactly that. You cannot stop taking medication after the symptoms have disappeared. This is a very dangerous habit and can lead to repeated illness and resistance of the bacteria or virus to drugs. Check with the prescribing physician if a drug needs to be given around the clock or only when the child is awake.

If a child looks and feels well and acts normally, you usually do not have to be as concerned with the presence of certain symptoms such as fever. The opposite is true also: If a child lacks obvious symptoms but does look, feel, and act sick, you should pay close attention to his complaints. Look at the total child and not just the specific aching part in evaluating an illness.

The contagious period of many illnesses starts *before* symptoms appear. Therefore it is almost impossible to prevent your child from being exposed to illness or from exposing others to his or her illness.

Do not use adult medicines for children unless you specifically check with your doctor first. Some adult medicines are *extremely* harmful to children, and some even have the opposite effect on children that they have on adults.

Clear liquids are recommended for many children when they experience stomach problems or nausea and vomiting. A clear liquid is any fluid that can be seen through, such as 7-Up, gelatin, and broth. It is best to give clear liquids at room temperature. If carbonated soda is given, let it stand and become flat before it is drunk.

Applying ice to a bruise or an affected area can be done by putting ice cubes in a plastic bag and applying it directly to the part, or by wrapping ice in a towel, or by using a frozen blue ice pack. In some instances, putting the affected part in a basin with ice and water is more effective. Ice bags can also be used.

There is no evidence that vitamin C prevents colds in children who are receiving an adequate diet. The routine administration of vitamin C may be helpful if you question your child's nutritional status. Vitamin C does not help in getting over a cold sooner. Foods high in vitamin C are citrus fruits and juices and fresh vegetables.

Keep the phone number of your family doctor and the local poison control center near each phone.

CHOOSING A FAMILY DOCTOR

Family practice is the one medical specialty where the physician can diagnose and treat a wide range of health problems in people of all ages, from newborn infants to the elderly. A family practitioner also delivers babies. For this reason many parents choose a family practitioner to be the doctor for the entire family rather than go to one doctor themselves and take their children to a pediatrician. The benefits of using a family practitioner include:

1. The physician gets to know the entire family, including the health history of all family members and any hereditary or recurring health problems.

2. Your children get to know and trust the physician over a period of many years—at least until they become adults, perhaps longer.

3. No transfer of records is necessary when the children become teenagers and no longer need or want to see a pediatrician.

4. The entire family can go for physical exams at the same time, and appointments can be scheduled back-to-back. This saves time and extra trips.

5. A family practitioner can handle all but the most severe medical problems.

Get a family doctor who understands your "working mother" schedule and problems. Then he might see your child early in the morning without a wait so you can still get to work on time (and get your child to school if he or she is well enough to go). Ask neighbors and friends whom you trust about their physicians. If they can highly recommend someone and have been with him or her for years, then this is a physician worth serious consideration.

A pediatrician is a specialist in caring for children and is certainly an option as a physician for your children.

While it is nice if your doctor's office is near your home, trust and reliability are far more important than location. You should feel free at all times to discuss any health problems or concerns you or your family may have, no matter how small or trivial they may seem; ask how a test or exam works, what it does, how it is helpful, and why it is necessary; ask for an explanation of a diagnosis; and request reassurance or explanation if something feels strange or inappropriate or contradicts your own information or observation.

You should intuitively feel that your family physician cares about your family's health. If you are unhappy with your physician's care, do not hesitate to find a new doctor.

SICK KIDS IN THE EARLY MORNING

If your child is ill, don't panic, but if he or she complains of illness in the early morning, a quick evaluation of the seriousness of the complaint must be done. Ask your child to describe symptoms in detail and check affected areas for soreness, heat, unusual color, limited movement, sensitivity, or pain when touched. If any of these items is present, you may need to call a physician.

If your child has a stomach complaint, sometimes going to the bathroom can alleviate the problem. If the child just isn't feeling well in general and is not sick to the stomach, breakfast may help in alleviating that sick feeling.

Observe your child's behavior. This is most important in evaluating the physical problems. A child who is acting quite normal but complaining a lot probably isn't as sick as the child who is acting sick with little complaining.

Staying home all day or going to work as usual is not your only option. Sometimes I call in late to work and stay with my child a few extra hours. This also allows me to take the child to the doctor or at least assess what his needs for the day will be. The more serious the early-morning symptoms, the more important this is, of course.

Open communication with your child is important. If the "illness" is caused by an anxiety-producing event at school, it is important to discuss this and (if possible) resolve the problem. You know your own child best, and intuition and judgment mean a lot in evaluating the seriousness of your child's complaint.

MEDICATIONS AND SUPPLIES TO HAVE IN THE HOUSE

Syrup of ipecac to induce vomiting in case of poisoning

Children's aspirin and acetaminophen to reduce fever and relieve assorted aches and pains (follow directions on the label for dosage and frequency according to your child's age)

Antibiotic ointment to help prevent infection from insect bites, cuts, and lacerations

Hydrogen peroxide, a disinfectant and antiseptic for cleaning scrapes, cuts, and lacerations

Decongestant to dry up mucus from the common cold (sometimes combined with antihistamines)

Calamine lotion to relieve itching of poison ivy and other rashes

Ointment to relieve diaper rash

Petroleum jelly to soothe dry skin and to prevent diaper rash

Saline nose drops to loosen nasal mucus

Soft drinks useful in relieving upset stomachs (diet soda should not be used)

Rectal thermometer for small children (until child can keep thermometer under his or her tongue)

Oral thermometer for older children

Sterile gauze pads in various sizes to cover wounds

Adhesive tape in assorted widths to attach sterile gauze

Band-Aids in assorted sizes and shapes

Bandage scissors for cutting bandages and adhesive

Tweezers and needles to remove splinters

Penlight to help examine a small area

Cotton swab applicators (Q-Tips, for example) for applying medications, removing particles from eyelids, etc.

Eyewash and eyecup

Elastic bandage for pressure dressing and to hold ice bag in place and provide support for a joint

Ice bag for bruises, breaks, sprains, and other injuries

Hot-water bottle to relieve stomachache or earache

Cold-mist humidifier to relieve sinus congestion (does not have a heating element so is safe near children)

Nasal syringe to extract mucus from the nose of an infant (parents are taught to use this before the mother leaves the hospital)

Keep medications and health supplies in one location for convenience and safety. When you run low on an item, be sure to replenish it.

COMMON HEALTH PROBLEMS

Following is an alphabetical list of symptoms of illnesses or injuries common among children. Under each heading are the categories General Information (including Precautions), Management, When to Call or See a Doctor, and School Considerations.

The symptoms may be associated with ailments other than those mentioned, and any one problem may have a wide range of symptoms. Only common childhood symptoms and management are detailed here. If you have any questions about your child's illness or if the illness seems serious or unusual, call your physician. Home treatment is for minor illnesses *only*.

These tips are not meant to replace the advice or diagnosis of a physician. They are general guides only and not procedures to be inflexibly followed. New methods and philosophies of care are being developed every day; check with your doctor if you question any suggestion presented here or if your children have chronic problems.

ALLERGIC REACTIONS

GENERAL INFORMATION

Sporadic allergic reactions are not unusual and should be differentiated from chronic allergies of children under a doctor's care. Symptoms include stuffy nose, asthmalike symptoms (for example, wheezing), and hives which appear anywhere on the skin and look like clusters of mosquito bites. An allergic reaction can be caused by nearly any food, drink, drug, or substance in the environment.

MANAGEMENT

Treat symptoms as they appear. Antihistamines, available over the counter, are helpful in relieving all symptoms of the allergic reaction. Cold compresses and calamine lotion are useful in relieving the discomfort of hives.

WHEN TO CALL OR SEE A DOCTOR

    If child has difficulty swallowing or breathing
    If itching interferes with sleep
    If the allergic reaction persists for several days without relief

SCHOOL CONSIDERATIONS

When the child is comfortable and is not having difficulty breathing or swallowing, school can be attended.

ANIMAL AND HUMAN BITES

GENERAL INFORMATION

These bites are significant only if the skin is broken. Human bites can cause more serious infections than those from animal bites, but make sure that the animal involved has had a rabies shot or is confined so it can be watched.

MANAGEMENT

Wash injury with soap and water. Keep the area clean and the bite covered with a clean dressing. Watch for symptoms of infection including fever, redness, pus drainage, or a red line extending from the injured area. Your child needs a tetanus booster if he or she has not had one within the past five years.

WHEN TO CALL OR SEE A DOCTOR

If the child has not had a tetanus booster in the last five years

At the *first sign* of infection

If the animal that bit your child cannot be identified or observed

If the initial injury is gaping open and needs stitches

SCHOOL CONSIDERATIONS

Child may go to school when he is comfortable and the injury is dressed.

BROKEN BONES

GENERAL INFORMATION

Any bone in the body can break. Symptoms include severe pain; dramatic swelling and bruising; instability, unusual flexibility, or movement of bone; deformity in the affected area, such as a finger or limb hanging at a strange angle; and limited ability to use the area or to bear weight on it. *Minor* breaks (where the bones are not out of position) may be treated initially with simple first aid. Further management can usually be delayed a few hours, if necessary.

MANAGEMENT

Support the broken bone so movement of the fractured part is minimized and apply ice to the affected area to reduce swelling and pain. If there is broken skin associated with the broken bone, it has to be treated immediately.

WHEN TO CALL OR SEE A DOCTOR

Anytime you suspect a broken bone.

SCHOOL CONSIDERATIONS

Once the break has been treated, the swelling has stabilized, and the child is comfortable, he or she can go to school. Your child may need to limit school activities, keep a part elevated, or use an elevator if available. This should be discussed with school officials.

BRUISES, LUMPS, AND BUMPS

GENERAL INFORMATION

The skin is intact in these cases but may be bruised, swollen, scraped, tender, and red or black and blue.

MANAGEMENT

Put an ice pack on the affected area within the first few hours and refresh frequently during the next forty-eight hours. Keep ice on for fifteen to twenty minutes at a time. See page 100 for instructions. An elastic bandage on a joint gives stability and helps prevent swelling. Give acetaminophen for pain, and elevate the affected area if possible.

WHEN TO CALL OR SEE A DOCTOR

If there is increasing swelling or pain after the first thirty-six hours

If the immediate pain is severe

If there is any sign of a broken bone (see "Broken Bones" above for symptoms)

SCHOOL CONSIDERATIONS

Your child can go to school when comfortable but should keep a bandage on the affected area both at home and in school, if so indicated by the physician.

BURNING ON URINATION

GENERAL INFORMATION

This problem is more frequent in girls than in boys. Teach girls to wipe themselves from front to back to help prevent this as wiping back to front provides a greater chance for infection. Girls can get vaginitis (inflammation of the vagina), which can cause pain on urination and may require treatment. Avoid use of bubble bath.

MANAGEMENT

Check your child's temperature and frequency of urination, urgency, and accidental wetting. Look at the color and consistency of the urine; pink-tinged or cloudy urine may indicate blood or albumin. Increase intake of fluids. In girls, apply soothing ointment to any rash around the vagina.

WHEN TO CALL OR SEE A DOCTOR

When pain on urination is accompanied by:

Fever of 101° or over

Pain in the back or abdomen

Bloody urine

If pain continues for several days or is associated with frequency, urgency, or accidents

If pain is severe

If your child has a previous history of bladder infections

If there is increased vaginal discharge

If you suspect an infection, take your child to the physician's office for a urine test. If this is not possible, obtain the specimen at home and deliver it to the physician yourself. In order to avoid a false positive result, sterilize the container or get a sterile container from your doctor. To take a specimen, wash the urethra and surrounding area with soap and water. Have your child urinate for several seconds *before* taking the sample. Usually about two ounces of urine is sufficient.

SCHOOL CONSIDERATIONS

If discomfort is tolerable and frequency is not a problem, your child can attend school. Your child may be put on medications and should continue on the schedule while attending school. This problem is not contagious.

BURNS

GENERAL INFORMATION

A first-degree burn is like a sunburn. A second-degree burn has either intact or broken blisters. A third-degree burn destroys the skin, which gets black and hard and won't grow back by itself.

MANAGEMENT

Do not put grease, such as butter, on a burn initially. Instead, apply cold water or ice to the burned area until pain stops. Second-degree burns should be washed with mild soap after applying ice or water (see page 100 for information on ice packs). Then apply antibiotic ointment and bandage with sterile gauze. Elevate the area if the burn is large.

WHEN TO CALL OR SEE A DOCTOR

If a burn has blistered and covers an area larger than the palm of your hand

If any area is hard, like leather, or brown or black in color or completely numb

If blisters become cloudy or look infected

Any third-degree burn should be seen by a physician

SCHOOL CONSIDERATIONS

Your child can go to school when he or she is comfortable and the burn area is covered with a dressing. Some activity restrictions may be necessary.

CONSTIPATION

GENERAL INFORMATION

Usually no treatment is needed for this disorder—it takes care of itself within a few days. Children are extremely different in their bowel habits, and some children are naturally irregular. Babies often grunt and turn red when having a bowel movement which is not pleasant-looking but is normal. Stress in children related to toilet training or bowel habits can cause constipation. Keep this in mind, and try not to become visibly concerned if your child is constipated, but be sure to observe the color and consistency of bowel movements.

MANAGEMENT

No treatment is often the answer. *Do not use* laxative or enemas without specific orders from your physician. Diet affects bowel habits; juice is helpful, as is fiber found in bran cereals, fresh fruits, and raw vegetables. Increase the child's fluid intake and allow plenty of uninterrupted time to have bowel movements.

WHEN TO CALL OR SEE A DOCTOR

If there is pain or cramps

If blood is seen in stools

If the condition persists more than a week

If your child is staining underpants often with little accidents

SCHOOL CONSIDERATIONS

Your child can go to school if he or she is not too uncomfortable. Constipation is usually not severe enough to keep a child at home.

COUGH

GENERAL INFORMATION

Coughing is a symptom of an irritation somewhere in the respiratory tract—the throat, esophagus, or lungs. Many coughs are caused by drainage from a cold. This is especially likely if the cough occurs during the night or when your child is lying down.

MANAGEMENT

Examine the coughed-up material and note the color. Check for associated symptoms such as fever or swollen glands. A decongestant and/or an antihistamine may be helpful. Have your child sleep on his stomach or propped up on his back with a cold-mist humidifier in the room to relieve congestion. Increase fluid intake to help loosen phlegm. Cough drops may be soothing; use a cough suppressant at night if your child is kept up by coughing spells.

WHEN TO CALL OR SEE A DOCTOR

If your child has a fever over 101°

If phlegm is yellow, brown, or bloody

If there is any difficulty breathing or if child is wheezing

If cough persists for five or more days with no other symptoms and without improvement

If cough exhausts your child and prevents sleeping or drinking

SCHOOL CONSIDERATIONS

If the cough is mild and associated with cold symptoms, and if your child feels well, school can be considered. However, your child should adhere to strict hygiene rules (see page 99). If cough is due to allergies, the school should be informed that the child is not contagious.

CUTS, WOUNDS, SCRATCHES, OR ANY BREAK IN THE SKIN

GENERAL INFORMATION

These are common in children and are usually not serious.

MANAGEMENT

If there is bleeding, apply direct pressure with a gauze pad or clean cloth, then wash the injury with soap and water. An ice application can reduce swelling (see page 100). Use hydrogen peroxide to cleanse old, dirty, or mildly infected injuries. Apply antibiotic ointment to prevent infection, then a dressing, either a Band-Aid or a gauze pad and tape.

WHEN TO CALL OR SEE A DOCTOR

If redness, warmth, or tenderness increases

If bleeding persists

If it is a gaping wound and may need stitches

If it is a dirty wound and your child has not had a tetanus shot within the last five years

SCHOOL CONSIDERATIONS

Your child can go to school once the injury is cleaned and dressed.

DIARRHEA

GENERAL INFORMATION

This condition is the repeated discharge of watery stools, usually several times a day. Color of stools can vary from light brown to green. This condition has many causes; look for other related problems. Diarrhea may cause abdominal cramps.

MANAGEMENT

Keep track of the number and consistency of bowel movements. Put your child's stomach at rest: Reduce food intake to clear liquids for twenty-four hours, then add bland foods until symptoms disappear. Then gradually resume regular diet. Substitute water for milk until the condition clears. Antidiarrheal drugs for children may be helpful.

WHEN TO CALL OR SEE A DOCTOR

If diarrhea is bloody or black

If diarrhea does not improve within twenty-four hours on clear liquids

If severe abdominal pain accompanies diarrhea

If signs of dehydration occur, such as decreased urination, no tears when crying, doughy skin, dry mouth, or a generally sick appearance

SCHOOL CONSIDERATIONS

Your child can go to school if the episodes of diarrhea are infrequent and if he feels good and wants to go to school. Your child should adhere to strict hygienic practices. Washing hands often is particularly important.

EARACHE

GENERAL INFORMATION

Earaches are common in young children because their eustachian tubes are narrow and easily blocked. Ear infections must be treated professionally and can occur without fever. Always check first to see if an object has been put in the ear. However, it is difficult to see beyond the opening and professional help will be needed to remove most objects stuck in the ear. If an eardrum breaks, fluid will leak out. This is not an emergency, but a physician should be notified. Often a broken eardrum will decrease the pain or may result in some blood.

MANAGEMENT

Check to see if there is increased pain when pulling the ear. This may indicate infection in the ear canal (swimmer's ear). Take your child's temperature every six hours and record it. Notice if pain is causing crying or complaining or other changes in your child's normal behavior. Infants and younger children may pull at an infected, painful ear. A hot-water bottle (with warm water) applied to an infected ear may decrease discomfort. A decongestant and/or antihistamine helps to relieve congestion in the middle ear and acetaminophen may reduce pain.

WHEN TO CALL OR SEE A DOCTOR

If your child's temperature is over 100.4° for forty-eight hours

If your child is three years old or younger (serious earaches are common in this age group)

If blood or pus drains from the ear

If pain continues more than twenty-four hours

If pain is increased when the ear is pulled

If dizziness is present

If a foreign object is in the ear and cannot be easily removed (if this is the case, *do not* continue to attempt removal)

SCHOOL CONSIDERATIONS

If the earache is mild, with no fever or other symptoms, your child may go to school. This is especially true if the child feels well or there are minor symptoms of a cold. Earache itself is not communicable. In deciding whether your child should go to school, focus on the underlying cause of the earache.

FEVER

GENERAL INFORMATION

Chills indicate that the temperature is going up. Your child's temperature should be taken at the end of an episode of chills. Sweating indicates that the temperature is coming down. Temperature normally varies with individuals and with the time of day. Rectal temperature is normally a degree higher than oral temperature; normal axillary (armpit) temperature is a degree below oral temperature. Temperatures a degree or so above or below normal (without accompanying symptoms) should not be cause for concern.

MANAGEMENT

Take and record temperature every four hours while the child is awake. Check frequently for associated symptoms such as an earache, sore throat, or swollen glands. Give your child acetaminophen. Insist on plenty of rest and increased normal fluid intake. A tepid bath helps bring down the temperature if medicines don't. Chills while bathing increase temperature, however, so if chills come on during the bath, get your child out of the tub.

WHEN TO CALL OR SEE A DOCTOR

If serious related symptoms occur

If low-grade fever (two to three degrees above normal) persists over a week

If fever is greater than 102° for three days

SCHOOL CONSIDERATIONS

If your child has a low-grade fever with no other symptoms and he or she feels good, you probably can send the child to school. However, the child might want to take a nap during the day. This may be possible in a day-care setting or latchkey program but if the child is of school age and feels tired during the day, encourage him or her to go to the nurse's office. Most schools have a cot where children can lie down. A child whose temperature is quite high or who doesn't feel well cannot be sent to school.

FOREIGN OBJECT IN EYE

GENERAL INFORMATION

Tearing is a natural occurrence and may help to wash the object from the eye. Discourage your child from rubbing the eye, as this can further irritate it.

MANAGEMENT

Examine the eye with a penlight. Look in the corners, where foreign bodies are frequently trapped. Look underneath the upper lid for a foreign body if one is not located in the corners. If you see something, remove it with a sterile cotton swab; if not, use an eyecup to wash out the eye. If the object is removed, but the sensation of a foreign body still persists, use an eye patch overnight.

WHEN TO CALL OR SEE A DOCTOR

If the foreign body can be seen and cannot be removed after several attempts

If an object is removed but the sensation of the foreign body persists after a patch has been worn overnight

If the sensation of a foreign body still exists after an eyewash even though it can't be seen

If the child has a history of eye problems

SCHOOL CONSIDERATIONS

Your child can go to school when the object is removed and he is comfortable, even if he is wearing an eye patch.

HEADACHE

GENERAL INFORMATION

Headaches are fairly common in children. They are sometimes caused by hunger, eyestrain, or stress, so check on these before seeking further evaluation or treatment.

MANAGEMENT

Determine whether the child has fallen or bumped his head, has a cold or other related symptoms, or is dizzy or confused. What is the location of the headache? Put a cold towel on the forehead and have the child rest and relax in a darkened, quiet room. Acetaminophen may help reduce discomfort.

WHEN TO CALL OR SEE A DOCTOR

If the headaches occur two or more times a week

If the headache is not relieved by acetaminophen and relaxation

If you cannot discover any cause
If the child shows signs of confusion or dizziness
If your child has had a head injury
If the pain is severe or accompanied by vomiting
If the pain involves only one side of the head

SCHOOL CONSIDERATIONS

If there is only a slight headache that is relieved by acetaminophen, your child may go to school. If the headache is persistent
or severe, keep your child out of school and find out the underlying cause.

INSECT BITES AND BEE, HORNET, AND WASP STINGS

GENERAL INFORMATION

Local skin reaction is similar for most types of insect bites. Swelling, which can be severe, usually occurs. Scratching can cause
infection. Allergic reactions usually develop only after repeated
bites. Try to prevent bites by encouraging your child to use insect
repellent when bugs are prevalent. When insects are especially
thick, encourage children to wear long pants and long-sleeved
shirts.

MANAGEMENT

Put ice on the bite immediately (see page 100). Oral antihistamines can help reduce itching and swelling. Meat tenderizer
placed on the bite will neutralize the reaction (this sounds silly,
but it is usually effective). Anti-itch lotion such as calamine can
be placed on the bite. Keep your child cool and comfortable.

WHEN TO CALL OR SEE A DOCTOR

If your child experiences an allergic reaction, he or she should be taken to the doctor or emergency room immediately. Signs of an allergic reaction include:

Swelling that is more than localized
Shortness of breath
Wheezing
Difficulty in swallowing
Swelling around face and eyes
Generalized body itch
Hives or a general rash all over the body
Dizziness, nausea, or abdominal cramps

SCHOOL CONSIDERATIONS

Your child can go to school unless an allergic reaction occurs.

MUSCLE AND JOINT PAINS

GENERAL INFORMATION

Children complain of leg and arm pain frequently. These pains may be significant when accompanied by swelling, redness, bruising, or fever, but more often they are harmless.

MANAGEMENT

Place a hot-water bottle or heating pad over the painful area. Give the child a hot bath and acetaminophen to relieve discomfort and have him rest the affected area.

WHEN TO CALL OR SEE A DOCTOR

If a joint has limited motion

If swelling or redness appears around a joint

If the severity of the pain increases over a period of three days

If pain interferes with normal functions—if it causes limping, for example

SCHOOL CONSIDERATIONS

Your child can go to school if the discomfort is not too great.

POISONING

GENERAL INFORMATION

Keep syrup of ipecac in the house, but don't use it without checking with a doctor or poison control center as there are some substances that should not be vomited. Keep the number of the local center near each phone. Poisoning is a common problem for children under five who like to taste things. "Mr. Yuk" stickers should be placed on all poisons and their meaning should be explained to children. The major sign of poisoning is a sick *or well* child with an empty bottle close at hand or with evidence of spilled substances on clothes or skin.

MANAGEMENT

Call the poison control center or your doctor first—*before* taking the child to the medical office or hospital. This allows you to begin following advice immediately: Time is of the essence. Identify what the poison is. Read the label (if available) and administer an antidote according to the label.

SCHOOL CONSIDERATIONS

Your child cannot attend school until the problem has been resolved.

RASHES

GENERAL INFORMATION

Rashes include flat red spots, raised lumps, and small blisters. They are common symptoms of many childhood diseases, both minor and serious ones, including measles and chicken pox. They can also be the results of simple irritations.

MANAGEMENT

Look for accompanying symptoms such as fever, sore throat, or insect bite. Note whether the rash is localized (in particular spots) or generalized (all over the body), is in the mouth or around the eyes, and is accompanied by itching. Are the red spots weeping or draining? Apply anti-itching lotion such as calamine and give cool baths to further relieve itching. Apply antibiotic ointment on skin broken from scratching. Take your child's temperature.

WHEN TO CALL OR SEE A DOCTOR

If the rash is not better within a week or if it continues to spread after several days

If there are indications of an accompanying disease

If itching is severe

If the rash involves the mouth, eyes, palms, or soles

SCHOOL CONSIDERATIONS

If open lesions are present, your child should not go to school, but if the child is comfortable and if the rash does not seem to be accompanied by other symptoms and is not due to a contagious disease, school can be considered.

RED EYE/PINKEYE (Conjunctivitis)

GENERAL INFORMATION

Conjunctivitis can be caused by bacteria, virus, allergies, toxic substances, or general irritation and may occur in one or both eyes. This condition may be highly contagious, so wash your hands *thoroughly* immediately after treating or touching the eye.

MANAGEMENT

Do not cover the eye with a patch or anything else. If a crust appears on the eye, wipe with a moist cotton ball or a soft, clean washcloth dipped in water. Eyedrops may be prescribed by your physician. Applying warm, wet compresses to the eye three to four times a day helps soften the discharge and brings blood to the area, which helps fight infection. Have your child prevent spread of the disease by following strict hygiene rules. Handwashing is especially important. Your child should avoid touching his eyes as much as possible. Whenever he does touch them, he should wash his hands immediately.

WHEN TO CALL OR SEE A DOCTOR

If the pain is more severe than just a scratchy or irritating feeling

If a discharge or pus is present

SCHOOL CONSIDERATIONS

Pinkeye due to infection is very contagious, and precautions should be taken to prevent it from spreading. Many school districts have a strict rule that children with pinkeye may not attend school. Spreading occurs if secretions from the eye are passed on to someone else's eye. This happens if a child rubs his eye and touches a toy, and then someone else plays with that toy and touches his own eye. If pus is present, the eye should be treated before the child goes to school.

RUNNY NOSE

GENERAL INFORMATION

This condition is caused by the common cold or allergy. It is usually a virus infection and antibiotics will not work, so do not use them if there are no other symptoms. Colds in children may last anywhere from three to ten days. There are over 200 cold viruses, and children will experience many colds. Both you and your child should take proper precautions against colds, but they simply cannot be avoided so learn to live with them.

MANAGEMENT

First take your child's temperature, look at the throat, and check glands for swelling. Acetaminophen may relieve discomfort or fever. Decongestants help dry up secretions but may make the child irritable; antihistamines will help relieve congestion but will cause drowsiness. Nonprescription nose drops may help loosen nasal secretions; put petroleum jelly on your child's nose to relieve soreness. A cold-mist humidifier in the child's room is helpful in relieving congestion. Remove mucus in infants with a bulb syringe. Raise the head of your child's bed for more comfort at night. Putting an extra pillow under the mattress is the easiest way to do this. Encourage more fluids than normal and plenty of rest.

WHEN TO CALL OR SEE A DOCTOR

If a runny nose is associated with other symptoms such as an earache

If a fever persists for forty-eight hours

If your child has difficulty breathing

SCHOOL CONSIDERATIONS

If your child has mild cold symptoms and feels well, he or she can go to school but must practice strict hygiene measures. You may want your child to continue decongestant medication so be sure to send medicine and a permission slip to school.

SORE THROAT (see also "Cough")

GENERAL INFORMATION

This is a frequent complaint of children with colds and is often associated with postnasal drip. This is most frequent in the morning or whenever children have been lying down for a period of time. Strep throat must be treated, but it is not an emergency. It is diagnosed by a simple throat culture that frequently can be taken at the physician's office by nonprofessional personnel and may not even require an appointment.

MANAGEMENT

Check the child's temperature and the lymph glands on either side of the neck. Run your fingers under the line of the jawbone to feel for enlarged, tender glands. With a penlight and the handle of a spoon for a tongue depressor, check the back of the throat for redness and check the tonsils for redness, white spots, and swelling. Have your child gargle with salt water. Mix one teaspoon of salt in a glass of warm water. Use an analgesic spray or lozenges to decrease pain. NOTE: Do not use these right before you are going to get a throat culture. Decongestant medication might help minor sore throats caused by postnasal drip. Juice and other cool liquids help relieve pain and acetaminophen can also relieve some of the discomfort.

WHEN TO CALL OR SEE A DOCTOR

> If accompanying fever persists for more than forty-eight hours
> If there are white spots on the tonsils
> If the glands are tender or swollen
> If your child has persistent, severe pain
> If there has been recent strep exposure
> If there is a history of repeated strep throats
> If there is a change in the quality of your child's voice
> If your child is unable to swallow solid foods or liquids

SCHOOL CONSIDERATIONS

If the sore throat is minor, you can send your child to school. However, he or she must maintain the strict hygiene rules outlined on page 99. If your child has a fever, he should stay home until his temperature is back to normal. Adequate treatment eliminates transmission of strep within twenty-four hours.

STOMACHACHE
(see also "Vomiting")

GENERAL INFORMATION

This is a common complaint in children but it can be serious, so you must pay attention to small details of the problem and its history.

MANAGEMENT

Note the history and progress of the pain: When did it first occur? Where in the abdomen is it? Is the area tender to the touch? Note the quality of the pain—is it sharp, burning, dull? Are there associated problems such as constipation, nausea, diarrhea, vomiting, loss of appetite, or urinary symptoms? Does the child have a fever or chills? Is the abdomen hard or enlarged, or does it look normal? When was the last time the child had a bowel movement? Is the child under stress? If there is no identifiable physical cause, ask your child if there is something worrying or bothering him.

Note the behavior of the child, whether he is acting normal or as though he is in pain. Find out what the child has eaten or swallowed in the past twenty-four hours. Strange, spoiled, or improperly cooked food may be responsible. Ask your child specifically if he or she has swallowed (accidentally or otherwise) any objects or other nonfood items.

Check your child's temperature. If nausea is present, no food or liquids should be taken; if not, maintain a clear-liquid diet. If your child is taking liquids, acetaminophen may be given to minimize discomfort. Rest may eliminate some of the pain.

WHEN TO CALL OR SEE A DOCTOR

If pain is severe, steadily increases, or is well localized

If your child's abdomen is tender with movement or to the touch

If vomiting, loss of appetite, fever, or diarrhea is present

If the pain persists three or more days

If your child has swallowed an object, anything poisonous, or anything not meant to be ingested

If there are associated urinary symptoms

SCHOOL CONSIDERATIONS

If it is a minor complaint with no other related symptoms and your child wants to go to school, let him or her go, but tell the child to call you and to tell the school nurse if the pain recurs or gets worse.

SWOLLEN GLANDS

GENERAL INFORMATION

Glands are also called lymph nodes. They swell and harden when an infection enters the body. Swollen glands are most noticeable in the neck so you should get a general idea of what the neck region of your child feels like when there is no swelling and your child is well so that you will be able to detect swollen glands easily.

MANAGEMENT

Check your child's temperature. Check the size of glands and see if they are tender. Feel the neck and along and under the jaw. Notice other related symptoms such as a cold or earache. Treat associated symptoms; there is no specific treatment for swollen glands but acetaminophen may help relieve discomfort.

WHEN TO CALL OR SEE A DOCTOR

If glands are large and very tender

If other significant symptoms are present

If enlarged glands continue for two weeks and are not associated with any obvious cause

SCHOOL CONSIDERATIONS

If your child feels well and the related symptoms are mild, he or she can attend school. Swollen glands in themselves are not contagious.

TEETHING

GENERAL INFORMATION

With the eruption of baby teeth, babies experience fretfulness, drooling, crying, sleep disturbance, and changes in eating habits. Teething can occur any time between birth and age two, and again after age five. Teething may cause a low-grade fever, may be associated with respiratory illness or diarrhea, or may cause discomfort in the ears.

MANAGEMENT

Give baby something to bite on—a teething ring, chilled pacifier, or teething biscuits. Acetaminophen may be helpful.

WHEN TO CALL OR SEE A DOCTOR

Doctors are not routinely seen for this problem.

SCHOOL CONSIDERATIONS

Your child can go to a babysitter or to day care but let the caretaker know that your baby is teething and may not act normally.

VOMITING

GENERAL INFORMATION

Usually accompanied by a feeling of nausea, vomiting is a common symptom often associated with another disease. The concern is not so much for the vomiting itself, but for the loss of body fluid and for the underlying problem.

MANAGEMENT

Take your child's temperature. Find out what your child has eaten or swallowed in the past twenty-four hours. Strange foods, strange combinations, or improperly prepared or spoiled food may be responsible. Ask specifically if your child has swallowed (accidentally or otherwise) any objects or other nonfood items. Restrict fluids and food. Your child should take absolutely *nothing* by mouth for four hours. Sips of clear fluids can be given if no vomiting has occurred for four hours. Gradually increase clear fluids if the symptoms do not reappear and add bland solid foods after twelve hours of no vomiting.

WHEN TO CALL OR SEE A DOCTOR

If vomiting continues after four hours of taking nothing by mouth

If symptoms of dehydration occur, such as scanty urine, dry mouth, lack of tears when crying, and doughy skin

If vomiting is accompanied by other symptoms such as abdominal cramps or diarrhea

If your child experiences confusion or lethargy, or sleeps more than usual for being sick

If your child has swallowed an object, anything poisonous, or anything not meant to be ingested

SCHOOL CONSIDERATIONS

Your child cannot go to school when experiencing nausea and vomiting.

ILLNESS DURING SCHOOL

Some schools have a registered nurse on duty at all times, some share a nurse with other schools, and still others may only have a health aide with minimal experience. You should find out what kind of health staff the school has when you register your child. All schools or school districts have policies regarding sick children and children who need to take medicine during school hours. These policies differ from district to district and sometimes from school to school. Familiarize yourself with your school's policy *before* your child gets sick and is affected by it. Question anything that is unclear and note how the rules will affect you and your child.

If your child has a chronic disease or condition, be sure his teachers and the school nurse are aware of his special health needs. If your child needs to take any medications at school, impress upon him the importance of taking the medicine regularly and at the proper time. If forms must be signed by a physician in order for medicine to be given to your child, keep some blank forms at home. Then if you need to take your child to the doctor in the morning, you can save a trip by having the doctor sign the permission form then.

Tell your child that if he is ill during school, he should go to the nurse or health aide, who will make a judgment on the seriousness of his symptoms. His temperature will be taken; anything over 100° will probably be considered a fever. If the symptoms seem serious enough—that is, if your child seems more than slightly ill—you will be called and asked to take him out of school. Explain this whole process to your child before school begins. In borderline cases, if the nurse or health aide knows a mother works, she may let the child stay in school. For this reason, let the nurse or aide know at the beginning of the year that you are a working mother. The school's concern is for the child. If your child visits the school nurse and is genuinely ill, you will always be called to pick him or her up from school.

Schools usually are not allowed to give children *any* medicines without a physician's permission slip. This includes aspirin and acetaminophen, but sometimes these may be given with the approval of a parent. You may wish to write a note at the beginning of the year allowing your child to take aspirin or acetaminophen in school whenever necessary. Most schools have beds or cots where children may lie down. Explain this to your child as well.

The school cannot release your child early unless you or your designee comes to pick him or her up. Be sure to set up a contingency plan for times when you cannot do this: Have a neighbor, relative, or other parent that does not work be "on call" for those times. Having two such people on call is even better, in case one is away when the call comes. Make sure your child and the nurse or aide have the phone numbers of both these people. Be specific on all emergency cards you fill out for school records. List your own work and home phone numbers, your husband's work number, and the numbers of your two on-call friends and neighbors. When any of this information changes, make sure your child and the school know.

CHILD-CARE OPTIONS FOR SICK KIDS

You will not always be able to stay home to care for your sick child —or you may not want to. If your child is seriously ill, you probably will want to (and should) stay home. In cases of less severe illness, however, it is important to arrange in advance alternative on-call child care. Here are some possibilities.

1. Neighbors may be willing to help once in a while and are a good backup source.

2. Formal babysitting services provide babysitters in the home on short notice. Check the Yellow Pages.

3. Relatives may be willing to help out in an emergency.

4. Often you can work out a backup exchange with other mothers. You can serve as a backup for them when you are not at work; in exchange, a mother who does not work herself can be your backup during your working hours.

5. High school or college students are usually willing to babysit for sick children if it doesn't conflict with their class schedules. This is particularly helpful on school holidays when you must work. Make sure the sitter and her parents know your child is ill.

6. Professional nursing personnel pools usually can provide in-home help ranging from a home-helper/aide to a professional nurse. This service is usually expensive, but in times of need it may be a viable option.

7. Some communities have child-care services geared specifically to care for a sick child in the home.

8. Know the grapevine—sometimes part-time sitters are available through church or neighborhood groups or through friends or friends of friends.

9. An older child might have to stay home with a younger child for a day or so if no other arrangements can be made. Be willing to keep the older child home from school to provide child care—older kids usually consider this a free vacation. However, use this option only as an infrequent last resort.

If you have to stay home, try to do some of your day's work at home. Perhaps you only need to stay home half a day and can find a babysitter for later in the day or after school. If necessary, alternate half days off with your spouse.

If your situation allows it, take your sick child to work with you. This is feasible if you have a private office where the child can lie down or play quiet games. This, of course, depends on your work situation and on the seriousness and contagion of your child's disease. Do not hesitate to stay home if you genuinely have to; keep your child's welfare foremost in your mind.

SICK CHILDREN AT HOME ALONE

A mature and responsible child with a minor illness may be able to stay home alone. The child should be at least ten to twelve years old. Have a neighbor look in every few hours and call you immediately if there is cause for concern. Call your child often and have your child call you if there are any problems. (Be sure he or she knows your work phone number and knows what you are called at work.)

Prepare and leave lunch, drinks, and a snack before you go. Be sure to leave diversionary activities—books, games, puzzles—so that your child need not rely too much on TV. Leave emergency numbers by the phone and use the same rules as those for children staying home alone after school (see Chapter 9, "School Days," page 147). Instruct your co-workers to get you immediately if your sick child calls you at work. Always inform them where you will be during each part of the day.

If your child is supposed to take medications by himself, let him practice taking the medicine while you are observing him. Be sure he understands the exact dosage and directions. Go over them carefully and ask him to repeat them to you shortly before you leave home. If possible, prepare individual doses in advance. Leave written instructions for your child to refer to if he forgets the directions or dosage. Call and check that the medicine has been taken correctly and at the right time.

9

School Days

BEFORE SCHOOL: EARLY-MORNING ORGANIZATION

This is usually one of the most hectic times of the day. If you and your children have difficulty getting out of bed in the morning or getting started, the entire family may dread mornings. As much as possible, try to get out of bed quickly and get moving. Not only does this save time, it keeps you from wanting to stay in bed and thus making yourself miserable.

Identify morning trouble spots and make adjustments. For example, if it takes a child fifteen minutes to get out of bed after being awakened, set his alarm for fifteen minutes earlier. If a child cannot make up his mind on what he wants to wear, either have him pick out his clothes the night before or pick them out for him. If a young child wants to choose his clothes, set out two outfits that mix and match the night before. This allows him a limited choice.

Have kids do as much as they can by themselves in the morning. They can comb their own hair; you only have to put on the finishing touches. They can put on their own shoes; you lace and tie, if necessary. Children can put on their own jackets so that you only have to zip up.

While children are getting ready for school, you can discuss the day's plans and expectations with them. Organize your house to encourage children to do things for themselves. Dishes should be low enough so children can reach them and breakfast cereal easy to find and reach. Getting the family up a bit earlier to allow some "wasted fun time" in the morning lifts everyone's spirits and gets them in a good mood for facing the day. These few minutes can easily be more rewarding (and may seem to last longer) than you would expect. Hugging and cuddling in bed before actually getting up and getting ready may be comforting and nurturing enough that the rest of the morning is more tolerable for everyone. Doing something relatively quiet together, such as walking the dog or listening to music or the news, can have a calming effect on the entire family.

Set a kitchen timer with a loud ticking sound and a bell to let kids know how long they have for each morning activity. For example, you might want to set it for five minutes for brushing teeth and fifteen minutes for getting dressed. This certainly helps the dawdlers. Make it into a game. Even young children understand trying to beat the bell, even if they can't tell time yet.

If you function better if you have some time for yourself in the morning, get up early—before the rest of the family—have a cup of coffee, read the paper, or take a shower in peace before the rest of the clan awakens. But have breakfast ready for children when they arrive at the table (see Chapter 14, page 180, for more on breakfast). Be sure all school items are packed and ready to go the night before. Bookbags or backpacks are helpful in transporting the many notes, papers, and projects to school and back. Lunch or milk money can be put in the bookbag in a small change purse. Having all this ready the night before makes the morning much less frantic. Also do as much as you can in preparing lunch the night before (see Chapter 14, page 184, for more on lunch).

You might want to role-play the morning routine once or twice before the actual school year starts. Young children find it difficult to understand time restraints, and a little practice beforehand might help. This is especially true if you are just coming out of a period (such as summer vacation) where there were no time restraints.

Everyone in the family should straighten up his or her own room—including the adults. Teach children early to assume this responsibility, and expect them to keep it up. You and your husband must set an example for them with your own bedroom, of course. Very young children cannot straighten up their own rooms, but you can teach them to help make the bed and eventually they can take over the task completely. Remember, it won't be perfect at first, but with repeated practice it will get better. The sooner you start training your children (and the more practice they get), the sooner they will be able to assume responsibility.

If you have to leave for work before school begins, read "Before- and After-school Alternatives," page 143.

ENLISTING THE SCHOOL'S ASSISTANCE

Very few schools understand working mothers. School systems in the past have expected a great deal from mothers in the form of volunteer work. Mothers were expected to volunteer for room duty, fund-raising events, and PTA, and were asked and expected to serve as teachers' aides, tutors, chaperones for field trips, chauffeurs, and any other jobs that came up. Now, not only aren't as many mothers volunteering, but many are not even available to fill most of the traditional expectations of the school system. Although many teachers are also mothers, the system for the most part has not recognized the working mother as a different being from the full-time homemaker. The system has remained to a large degree unaware of the working mother's commitments and duties.

Before your child is even old enough to attend public school, become active in your school system. Go to school board meetings and get on mailing lists to receive information. This will help orient you to the practices and philosophies of your particular school district. Begin presenting your views at meetings early. Point out expectations that are excessive or inappropriate for two-career parents. Organize a group of working mothers to find, research, and present alternatives to practices and traditions that demand daytime hours of mothers. Present alternatives of your own.

It is worth getting involved in a few school activities. Evening meetings may be possible if the time commitment is limited. By getting involved in the right committee, you may even be able to help set policies more beneficial to you, your family, and other dual-career and single-parent families.

When your child begins school (and each subsequent September) notify his or her teacher that you are a working mother. This can be done through a note, a telephone call, or a friendly conference over a cup of coffee. Let the teacher know your exact situation, including the hours you work and what it is that you do. Impress upon her that although you are a working parent you are quite concerned and involved with your child. Let the teacher know your phone number at work and/or where you can be reached during the day. Stress that you don't mind being called at work for anything important and that being called won't jeopardize or interfere with your job. Give the teacher your home telephone number and invite her to call you in the evening with any problem or question. Inform the teacher if any major changes occur at home. For example, if you have to go out of town for a few days or if your work schedule changes, there might be a change in your child's schoolwork or behavior in class.

Be appreciative for any extra attention your child receives at school. Giving small Christmas presents (if not prohibited) is an appropriate way of thanking teachers. If you have established a good relationship with your child's teacher, he or she may serve as a great support in a time of crisis.

Be sure to fill out emergency cards completely and accurately. Obtain a school calendar at the beginning of each school year and note school closures for holidays, conferences, workshops, etc. Prepare for these days far in advance. Sign up for parent-teacher conferences well in advance also. Use early-morning, evening, or late-afternoon slots. If timing cannot be worked out, have a telephone conference. This is perfectly satisfactory if your child is not experiencing (or causing) any problems. Before you go to a conference with your child's teacher, ask your child if he or she is having any problems or wants any questions answered. Be sure to discuss these with the teacher and then with your child.

Let the teacher know that you need plenty of advance notice for class plays, trips, or meetings that occur during your regular working hours. Discourage any midafternoon parent-child activities such as plays or outings. Sometimes just making the teacher aware of the problems such an activity can cause is enough to end it before it begins. This is especially true for the 10:30 A.M. kindergarten Christmas play. You might have to drive an hour each way to attend a half-hour play, only to cause tears when your child cannot go home with his mom like the other kids.

Contingency plans must be made for unplanned school closings due to snowstorms and other emergencies. Often a neighbor's teenager can watch the kids, since his or her school will also be closed. Teenagers will also usually be available to watch your children on days when the public schools are closed because of teachers' meetings, conferences, and so on.

Try to get to know the teachers at the school. Request teachers for your children who are working mothers themselves or who otherwise understand your situation. Usually you can find out who these teachers are with a little selective questioning of other parents. Visit with these teachers; discuss your working-mother situation and try to get a feel for each teacher's ability and empathy. Then make your request for the following year.

If you have children at two or more schools, be extra careful of how you commit your time. Each school will be asking you to serve on committees, work as a volunteer, and so on, doubling or tripling the number of requests. Be especially selective in the tasks you agree to take on, and be aware that you will have to turn down twice as many as you accept. Try not to rock the boat too much in one year. Traditions are difficult to break, and many people (including those who run schools and school systems) need time to adjust even to small, necessary changes.

SPECIAL PROBLEMS OF THE KINDERGARTEN YEAR

Kindergartens typically run for two and one half hours. The day is usually divided into two half-day sessions. Morning kindergartens usually run from about 9:00 to 11:30 A.M., and afternoon kindergartens usually run from around 12:30 to 3:00 P.M. Your five-year-old will attend one of these sessions daily. Either session presents problems for almost every working mother.

Child-care arrangements must be made for the child for the morning or afternoon; in addition, you will need to arrange transportation to and from school. You should do both before school officially begins. Many kindergartens have an initial get-together the April or May before the school year begins. This is an excellent opportunity to begin formulating plans. Sometimes mothers who do not have full-time jobs and have kindergarteners themselves do not mind caring for another kindergarten child for a few hours a day. This provides a playmate for their own child and little extra work for them. (Remember, the children must be on the same kindergarten schedule.)

Call the school to request babysitting assistance. Sometimes the secretary in the main office keeps a list of mothers interested in babysitting, and/or a list of available sitters and other day-care situations. If she does not keep such lists already, suggest that she do so.

Often the school does not want to get involved in making babysitting contacts. However, you can obtain a list of all the kindergarteners yourself and mail out letters to their families asking for babysitting assistance. Be sure to write to mothers of children in all the kindergarten classes, not just your child's class. This is worth doing several weeks before the school year begins.

It is sometimes possible to move your child to a different session for babysitting reasons. This becomes more difficult if the class is large or if one session has many more children than the other.

If your child rides a bus to kindergarten, special arrangements must be made for him to ride a different bus from the one he is scheduled for. This may also be necessary if your child spends part of the day at a day-care center or at the home of another family or if he needs to go somewhere other than home after school. Making this arrangement usually is not a problem.

All-day kindergartens are beginning to be set up around the country. These usually run for six hours and/or follow the regular school schedule. These full-day sessions are ideal for families with working mothers, and the popularity of such programs shows that they are responsive to the needs of modern families. The increased school hours better enable teachers to serve the curiosity and developing intellect of sophisticated, energetic, and eager five-year-olds. The full day also allows for more field trips, films, and other activities.

Parents need to become involved with the school and school policy if they wish to encourage the development and continuation of all-day kindergartens. Get to know the school principal and other high-level decision-makers (such as assistant principals and school board members) and let them know how useful and important all-day kindergartens are to you. If possible, volunteer for an appropriate committee, perhaps one that helps set kindergarten or school policy. Parents must stay involved to assure that all-day kindergartens do not disappear as school budgets continue to tighten up. A small fee is sometimes charged for all-day kindergartens, usually far lower than that charged for any private alternative.

Private all-day kindergartens are another option. Take care in selecting a satisfactory school; you can use many of the techniques described in Chapter 4, "Choosing Day Care," page 69. These schools can be costly but are usually worthwhile. Be sure transportation does not cause a problem.

Church or community groups sometimes can meet your family's needs for the kindergarten year. If enough children need care (usually six to ten), you can often request a community group to organize some appropriate program for them.

Latchkey programs are all-day school programs for kindergarten and school-age children. (The term *latchkey* refers to the key worn around the neck of children who come home to an empty house after school.) These programs are sponsored by the school system or by the community and are supported by parent fees. They are usually housed right in the school buildings, and regular bus service is normally available. These programs are not extended kindergartens; the activities are primarily for entertainment and not for education. Latchkeys are open from 7:00 A.M. to 6:00 P.M., and youngsters are kept busy with fun activities until parents pick them up. Transportation has to be arranged if hours are earlier or later than the usual bus times. Latchkeys usually consist of three separate sessions: before school; after and/or before kindergarten; and after regular school. Costs vary, depending on the services provided and the number of hours your child spends there daily. Breakfast and lunch are normally provided at your option. Some parent involvement is usually desired.

Some day-care centers have kindergarten sessions that children can attend before or after regular kindergarten. If your center or babysitter is in the same school district as your home, regular school bus service can be provided directly from the school to the center or sitter's home, or vice versa. This may take some prearranging with the school but should not be a problem. If the day-care center or babysitter is not in the same school district, other transportation arrangements must be made. Some babysitters will agree to pick up children, or a neighbor or relative might agree to this responsibility.

Private schools sometimes have extended after-school hours as well.

If your child walks home from kindergarten or from an after-school activity, be sure he knows the way. Have him memorize your work phone number in the event he does get lost or in case of any other emergency. Be sure the school authorities know exactly where your child comes from when he arrives at school, and where he goes when he leaves. The authorities should also know what form of transportation he uses and who is responsible for it. All this information can be crucial in an emergency.

BEFORE- AND AFTER-SCHOOL ALTERNATIVES (Ages 5–11)

Most jobs begin at or before 9:00 A.M. and extend well beyond 3:00 P.M. This means some child-care arrangements must be established for children before and after school. For the young child, this means *organized, supervised* care such as the latchkey programs, day-care centers, and private sitters just described. In any of these arrangements, you can drop your child off on the way to work and pick him or her up on your way home. Try to make arrangements for both before and after school prior to the start of the school year. This saves a great deal of hassle.

Neighbors or relatives who have school-age children on the same schedules as yours may be willing to care for your children before or after school. Since they have to be home for their own children anyway, the extra child (or children) may not create a problem. Also, your and their children can play together. If you cannot make such an arrangement with a friend, call the school and get a list of the parents of all the children in your child's grade (not just his or her particular class). Chances are good that you can work something out with one of these families. You can either make your inquiries by phone or send out a form letter asking for assistance. This can (and ideally should) be done before the school year begins. You are not strictly limited to parents of children in the same grade as your child, of course. Your chances of finding a neighbor, other parent, or relative to look after your child increase if you can offer something in return. Often this is money, but it could also be some professional service or favor.

A babysitter coming to the house in the morning and after school is one of the most convenient ways to solve the early-morning and after-school problem. Teenagers, preteens, or even fifth- and sixth-graders in the neighborhood who attend the same or a nearby school may be willing to get the kids ready for school, feed them breakfast, get them to the bus or to school, and babysit after school for an hourly fee.

An older boy or girl might be willing to mind a child in his or her home, rather than yours. You would then have to drop your child off in the morning and/or pick him up in the evening, but this may still be fairly convenient. Licensed babysitters are usually willing to watch children before school, feed them breakfast, and get them on the bus or to school. A nearby day-care center may do this also.

If the time you leave in the morning is close to the time your child leaves, he may be able to care for himself if he is seven or older. The child must be responsible enough to get himself ready and out of the house safely, on time, and properly dressed for the weather. He must also always remember and be able to lock the door behind him. This applies for the after-school hours also. See "Children Staying Home Alone," page 147, for details.

There are usually quite a few community-sponsored after-school programs offered at various times. City parks and recreation departments, local Y's, church groups, and athletic leagues offer a variety of after-school activities. The major drawback of such short-term programs is that when they end, you must make new arrangements for your child.

Always have transportation plans for getting your child to and from school and to and from after-school activities. Arrange them beforehand and write them down. Your child should have specific instructions and know exactly how he or she will be getting to and from each activity. He should go home right after an after-school activity unless he has gotten permission to go somewhere else. If it is dark, arrangements should be made to have him picked up. If your child walks to or from an activity, be sure he knows the way.

EXTRACURRICULAR ACTIVITIES

Selecting and scheduling your child's extracurricular activities must be done with consideration for both your child's and your own needs. *Don't overdo it!* This is not healthy for your child, yourself, or your relationship. Frequently working parents schedule more activities for their children than necessary out of guilt or worry that their children are missing out. Try to avoid this.

Investigate activities that are convenient and compatible with your family's life-style and interests. Then discuss these with your youngsters and decide on ones desirable to *all* concerned. If two children can participate in an activity occurring at the same time in the same place, this becomes extremely attractive. For example, a music school might have simultaneous lessons for children of varying ages and abilities. (This may give you some free time while they are busy.)

In choosing activities for children, be sure they are worth the effort of getting to them. A fifteen-minute music lesson that you have to drive forty-five minutes to get to may just not be worth it, no matter how good the teacher is. Needless to say, your child should participate in activities he enjoys. Do not pressure him into taking part in something he would rather avoid but it is all right to make suggestions, of course.

Children do not have to take lessons in everything. You may wish to encourage them to try several different things at first, but do not push them to do this. Eventually they will select one or two things that they want to concentrate their effort on; let them stick with these.

Violin lessons are not "better" for your child than playing on a local baseball team, or vice versa. What is important is whether your child enjoys and appreciates the activity. Children do not have to take lessons in something to learn it or to become good at it. Many skills and interests develop on their own, simply out of experience and going to school. These skills are as enjoyable and rewarding as those where formal guidance is provided—sometimes more so, because there is no pressure to perform in a certain way. Allow your children plenty of time and opportunity for these nonorganized activities.

Saturdays are excellent for activities. However, be careful not to overburden your children. Many birthday parties, trips and outings (to zoos, museums, parks), and other special activities are scheduled on Saturday also. Leave your children enough time to play with their friends or by themselves—or to do nothing. They need this kind of time just as you do.

Activities that take place at or near school should be encouraged. You then only have to worry about getting your child home. If your child must walk home from an activity after dark or through an unsafe neighborhood, it is always best to have an adult walk home with him or her.

Scheduled times for activities are not always convenient; however, if you can get enough children together to make up a class or group, the teacher or leader will often let you establish your own time. Usually this can be done with as few as six or eight kids.

Older children can make their own arrangements for after-school activities. They can work out the details by themselves and present the whole plan to you for discussion and approval. This is not only helpful and convenient for you, but it teaches kids to be self-reliant and responsible. Ideally, older children will make their own transportation arrangements as well, but unfortunately you will wind up driving them around all too often, so don't expect too much. By the time your child is fourteen or so, he can be left to his own devices. When he needs your help with an activity, encourage him to ask for it.

In some areas, there are commercial after-school clubs similar to day camps. These clubs provide lessons in ice skating, music, dance, and so on. Although these may be convenient, they can be expensive.

Make the organizers or coordinators of your children's after-school activities aware of the problems, time restraints, and schedule you have as a working mother. Encourage them to revamp their activities schedule to accommodate children from dual-career and single-parent families. Sometimes enough requests from parents will get schedules changed; other times, schedules will change of necessity as enrollments in inconveniently timed activities decline.

Discourage television as an activity except when special or educational programs are on.

CHILDREN STAYING HOME ALONE

Leaving your child alone after school is an alternative if the child is responsible and self-reliant. A child must agree to and *want* to stay home alone before this should be considered. If your child is willing to stay home alone but is not enthusiastic about it, that is all right; under no circumstances, however, should he or she be pressured into doing it.

Children generally can stay at home alone regularly by the age of ten or eleven, depending on several factors:

Maturity and dependability of the child

Safety of the neighborhood

Safety of your home (if your home is not very safe, *make* it safe as quickly as possible—see pages 98–99)

Cooperation of neighbors

Number of children staying together, and the degree to which they get along

The length of time the child will be alone

Allow your child to stay alone for an hour or so at first. Then try it for a few days in a row and if he tolerates this well, gradually increase the number of hours.

Your child should practice using the key to lock and unlock the door by himself. The key to the house should be secured to his clothes or hung around his neck on a string. You might consider hiding another key somewhere outside the house or leaving one with a neighbor in case your child still manages to lose it. Be sure to impress upon your child the importance of locking the door and checking to make sure it is indeed locked each time he leaves the house.

The house should provide a safe environment for your child:

1. Smoke alarms should be placed in strategic points.
2. A flashlight should be handy and in working order (check

it occasionally). Make sure your child knows where to find it.

3. Fire drills should be practiced by the whole family.

4. Visible, easily read emergency telephone numbers should always be posted near at least one phone, preferably near each phone. (See pages 150 and 151 for a sample list of important phone numbers.)

5. Any firearms should be locked away out of children's reach.

6. All poisons should be labeled and put out of children's reach also. Use "Mr. Yuk" stickers.

7. The entire family should review and *practice* what to do in the event of an emergency (such as an injury or sudden illness or a break-in). *Rehearse* the procedures with your children—just telling them is not enough.

Special rules and regulations are usually necessary for when a child is home alone. Some common rules are:

1. No company is allowed in the house unless prior permission has been given. This applies to both strangers and friends.

2. When answering the phone, never say your parents are not home. Say something like, "My mom can't come to the phone right now; can she call you back?" Then take a message.

3. Some parents do not want their children to answer the phone at all when they are not home and devise a signal system for when they call. For example, this may be an initial three rings, then a one-minute wait, then another ring.

4. Never open the door for anyone unless you are expecting them. Tell the child if someone is expected and give directions on what to do.

5. Do not use any electrical equipment, matches, or the stove. Normal exceptions to this rule are the TV, radio, and record player.

6. Call parents or a designated adult if anything unusual occurs.

General guidelines should be set for rooms the child can play in as well as snacking, TV, homework, and chores. If more than one child is left alone, strict rules should be set and enforced on how to get along and how to settle differences. All the regular house and family rules should continue to apply when adults are not at home.

Instructions for shutting off water, electricity, the heating system, and other major household systems should be left in a convenient, safe place where your child can get to them if necessary.

Have your child call you when he or she gets home. If you have more than one child, have them wait until they all get home to call. Let friendly neighbors know your child is home alone so they can watch out for any emergency and check on the child occasionally. Leave a loving note and a snack for your child each day.

If two children are home alone, it may be better not to leave one of them in charge, but to make each child responsible for him or herself. The major exception is when one child is several years older than the other. If one child is older and is in charge, clear expectations and rules must be established regarding his responsibility for (and authority over) the younger child. Many children do not want a babysitter after school and will obey household rules when home alone just to keep you from hiring one.

Things to check on to determine if your children are happy while they are home alone:

1. Are your children relaxed and comfortable when you get home?
2. Do they call you too frequently at work?
3. Are house rules and regulations being maintained?
4. Were they busy with safe and useful activities? (You may have to settle for safe and useless activities much of the time.)
5. Were required chores accomplished?
6. Did your children react appropriately to any unusual situation?
7. Did siblings resolve differences in a satisfactory manner?

One of the main reasons that children staying home alone works is that parents have confidence in their children and in this particular arrangement. Many positive qualities develop early in children because they are allowed to be responsible for themselves. Many of the problems and accidents that occur would have occurred even if you had been at home, and learning to face and deal with these at a young age helps children become more secure and trustworthy. But do not ask your child to assume more responsibility than he or she can handle. If a task or responsibility appears to be too much for your child, wait a few weeks or months before you suggest it again.

Here is a sample list of numbers to keep by the phone:

IMPORTANT PHONE NUMBERS

Mom at work _____

Dad at work _____

Neighbors: Mrs. Canby _____

Mrs. Jones _____

Mrs. Smith _____

Police Department _____

Fire Department _____

Family doctor, Dr. Brown _____

Dentist, Dr. Rosen _____

Poison control center _____

Relatives: Grandma _____

Aunt Rita _____

Aunt Dotty _____

Ambulance _____

Hospital _____

DIRECTIONS FOR MAKING AN EMERGENCY CALL

1. Be calm.
2. Give your name, address, and telephone number slowly and clearly.
3. Explain the kind of emergency you are reporting.
4. Do not hang up until you are told to by the person you are talking to, or until he or she hangs up.
5. If you are calling a doctor or dentist, talk to the person who answers the phone even though this may not be the doctor.

10

School Vacations

Children are out of school for a variety of reasons—holidays, teacher conventions and conferences, winter and spring breaks, and summer vacation—and preplanning for child care is crucial for such times. Obtain a list of school holidays at the beginning of the year and mark dates on your calendar. Begin planning well in advance. Compare local junior high, high school, and college holidays with those of your child; if they are the same you can enlist these students as babysitters.

If possible, plan family vacations for these times so that your child will not have to miss school for vacations and you will not have to arrange child care. Try to take personal days or vacation days when children are off from school, especially when they have single days off. This makes those days special for all concerned.

Day-care centers may take children for an individual day or week of a school vacation. If your child is responsible enough to arrange his own activities during vacations, let him—with your consultation and approval. If it's a one-day vacation, you may be able to take your child to work with you. Be sure this is agreeable to both your employer and your child: A bored and unhappy child can make a whole office miserable.

Options for the summer include summer school, neighborhood-supported activity centers, Y's, and summer play school. However, these activities do not run all day and other arrangements have to be made for off hours. Some day-care centers are open year round or you might hire a live-in mother's helper.

Usually mother's helpers are high school girls who want a job and a place to live during the summer months. The best way to find them is through newspaper ads in small-town papers or in a large city newspaper's rural edition. College students are sometimes interested in being mother's helpers, also. Follow the same rules for hiring summer help as for other hired help (refer to Chapter 5 for more information).

Summer days can be long, no matter how creative a babysitter is, and prearranged activity can be a lifesaver. Some special activities include:

A long walk with a canteen of water or Kool-Aid

A picnic in the park

Cooking or baking something special for the family

Having friends over (this must be cleared with both sets of parents)

Planting, weeding, or harvesting a vegetable or flower garden

Running a lemonade stand

Building a treehouse or fort (or some other building project)

Sewing something special

Making a tent playhouse to stay up all summer

Organizing neighborhood games such as jump rope, softball, or kickball

Taking a city bus to the library, movie, zoo, museums, or other city attractions

Be sure to reimburse the helper for any cash outlay in connection with your family. Evaluate how the summer is going periodically. Sit down and talk to the kids privately, then to the helper. You should never feel that you don't have other options and that you are stuck with a poor situation. Be willing to make changes, even drastic ones (such as firing the mother's helper), if they are called for. Be friendly but don't get too involved with your helper's private life. She is only with you for a few months and you should not assume the role of a mother substitute.

DAY CAMP

All major cities have day camps. They are sponsored by Y's, churches, and private and community organizations. Check with neighbors, kids, area organizations, churches and synagogues, and your local library for names of some local ones.

Hours are usually from 8:00 A.M. to 4:00 P.M. Bus transportation is usually provided, either from a centralized pick-up point or from your door. Make sure transportation to and from the camp is convenient. Lunch either is provided by the camp or must be brought from home. If packing lunches is a problem, look for a camp that provides a meal. Activities usually include sports, arts and crafts, various skill developments such as archery or canoeing, and sometimes music and dance. Academics are usually not part of the schedule unless it is a special camp program.

Day camps should be checked and investigated just as other child-care centers are. Check references, the facilities, supervision, and the environment before making a decision.

SLEEPAWAY CAMP

Emotionally mature children of six or older can usually attend sleepaway camp. Some camps have children well into their teens. Sessions usually run from one to eight weeks. One or two weeks is usually long enough for young first-time campers. Costs vary a great deal from camp to camp.

To find a good camp, talk to other parents and neighbors, physicians, school officials, community centers, and your chamber of commerce, or write to the American Camping Association at Bradford Woods, Martinsville, Indiana 46151. Special camps are available for athletics, science, arts and music, and for children with chronic diseases or handicaps.

Camps should be contacted in January or February for attendance the following summer. Ask yourself what you want your child to get out of camp to help narrow down the type of camp you select for your child. Do you want a large multifaceted camp or a smaller camp? a religious-affiliated camp or a general camp? Write to camps for literature and pictures. If possible, visit with your child before making a final decision. Talk to the director about the ratio of children to adults, ages and qualifications of counselors, types of activities, amount of free or nonstructured time, rules and regulations, medical care, food, religious activities, and other concerns. Try to get a feel for the staff and for the camp as a whole; remember, your intuition is important. Call previous campers and talk to them and their parents to get a realistic picture of the camp.

All children are apprehensive at first. Many fears stem from worry about making friends. These fears and homesickness usually last one or two days and are then forgotten. Parents should be sympathetic to fears and anxieties but should not change plans because of momentary resistance on the part of the camper.

Find out when visiting day is well in advance so you can be present that day. It is important to visit your children to show them you continue to love them and think about them. Be sure to write frequently to your children at camp.

Camp can be a positive experience for children and is an excellent option for working mothers during summer vacation. If your child simply does not enjoy camp the first time, however, it is best to find some other summer activity for the next few years.

11

Getting Around

In cities where public transportation is available, families may choose not to own a car. This has its advantages as it eliminates the costs and mechanical problems associated with car ownership but can cause problems if public transportation is not readily available and reliable.

Having only one car can work out if schedules are compatible and if both (or all) drivers agree to certain compromises. For example, one adult can drop off another before work and pick up after work.

Two or more cars usually allow for independent transportation of parents and more flexibility of schedules; however, alternatives must be available for those inevitable times when the car breaks down or is being serviced.

Public transportation has its advantages:

1. You may be able to snooze or rest while traveling.
2. The ride may give you time to prepare for the day, read, or relax before work begins.
3. No worry about parking and tickets.
4. You may actually save time since public transportation may be able to use special traffic lanes or a more direct route.

and its problems:

1. It may be running late.

2. You have limited flexibility in going to unscheduled locations.
3. It may take longer if there is no direct route to your destination.
4. The bus or train might be crowded with no seat available.
5. It may be noisy and impossible to read or relax.
6. Strikes by transportation workers seem to occur routinely
   in some cities.
7. In many locales you need to have correct change.

In driving your own car, traffic and parking are the major disad-
vantages. If possible, your own rented parking space saves time
and headaches if the cost is not prohibitive.

TRANSPORTATION FOR KIDS

Assuring your children's transportation to and from scheduled
appointments and activities is a major concern for all working
mothers. As children get older, their transportation needs become
more complex and need more creative solutions. Well-made advance plans are the best bet for accommodating everyone's particular needs and desires.

Hiring a teenager who drives and has a car can work well. It
is a must that this person be responsible and mature. Always
check references. Other persons you can hire for chauffeuring
duties include retirees, housekeepers, and college students.

Encourage children to use city buses or subways, when safe. If
your children are younger than eight or nine, you can hire a
teenager to escort them on the bus to and from activities. Many
cities require exact change for public transportation so be sure you
have an ample supply of coins. Keep current bus, subway, and
train schedules in a convenient place.

Give (or leave) explicit directions for public transportation. For
example, include the location of the bus stop, the number of the
bus, the destination stop, how to get to the activity from the bus

stop, etc. Be sure children know what to do if they get lost. Let them know you may be late in picking them up sometimes due to weather conditions, traffic, or last-minute telephone calls. Tell them not to worry and assure them you will call if any major change in plan occurs. Then do call if you expect to be more than fifteen minutes late.

Review safety precautions for traveling in a city, including never talking to strangers, going straight to an activity and home again, following traffic signals and rules, and knowing what to do if a bus is missed or late. Give children emergency telephone numbers to carry with them in case something happens, and money to pay for the call. Tell them not to use this money except for emergencies.

If other adults pick your children up from day care or other after-school programs, be sure to let the staff know. Many programs have strict rules regarding whom children may leave with.

If you take the bus or public transportation yourself, be sure your child's day care or activity is conveniently located in relation to your travel needs. Taking public transportation with your child can be a good experience; since you do not need to concentrate on driving, you can concentrate on your child and use the time for reading a story aloud, reviewing schoolwork, or talking together.

Arranging ideal (or even any) transportation for certain activities simply may not be possible, and sometimes you just won't be able to accommodate everyone. Sometimes, too, the best of plans will go awry. Don't let these things disturb you too much, and teach your children to accept these occasional disappointments.

CAR POOLS

To ensure smooth functioning of car pools, have a master list of driving schedules made up far in advance and copied for each parent. Be sure to include telephone numbers of all participants. A nonworking parent can drive kids to an after-school activity and a working parent can pick up. Or alternate weeks with all the parents in the car pool so that one person is responsible for picking up and dropping off the kids all week. That way, if five kids are in the car pool you will only have to drive every fifth week, and you may be able to fit that into your work schedule. Have emergency backups for your turn car-pooling. Be flexible. Many times emergencies happen and someone can't drive. Don't get turned off to car pools just because of one or two problems which can usually be resolved with a little effort.

If you are looking for a car pool, put an ad in an area newsletter asking people who live in your neighborhood to contact you if interested. Other places to advertise include neighborhood bulletin boards and church or club newsletters. If you are in more than one car pool, be sure you have an accurate calendar so you can keep the dates and locations straight. When forming the car pool, get all the participants together over coffee one evening. Have them bring their calendars. This helps planning go smoothly and easily and minimizes misunderstandings. If you have a good experience with the members of your car pool, keep in touch with them and make efforts to schedule your children's activities with theirs.

If several children in the same neighborhood need transportation, they can share a cab. This is usually expensive but does perform the service in a crunch and is a form of carpooling. Have an emergency plan set up in case you can't pick up your child or the car-pool children at the prearranged time. Neighbors or relatives may be willing to help you out in a pinch.

Having neighborhood children attend the same babysitter or day care is convenient because it allows car-pooling. However, this is sometimes difficult to arrange and may not be desirable if children are infants or toddlers. Preschoolers usually don't mind being driven by people other than their parents.

CAR TIPS

Even if you make great car-pooling arrangements, you will still spend a lot of time in the car, driving kids to school, picking them up, or chauffeuring them to different lessons or activities. Use this time with kids to the best advantage but maintain safety standards. Seat belts should always be worn by *all* passengers (adults and children) and by the driver. To assure that belts are worn, do not start the car until everyone has buckled up. Allow no exceptions to this, including—especially—yourself. All infants should travel in special car seats to protect them in case of a collision or a sudden stop. Always have the following items in the car:

Towelettes
Tissues
Trash container
Extra diapers for infants
Flashlight (check it occasionally to make sure it still works)

If you pick up children from more than one school, try to alternate who gets picked up first. This allows you to spend some individual time with each child. For longer car rides, special car toys help occupy children's time. Car toys should be safe, self-contained, and quiet. They should not be able to spill or ruin seat covers or clothes, and should be big enough so they don't get lost in the seat. Car toys should not come apart (by design or accident) into lots of pieces and should be able to be enjoyed in the confines of a seat belt. Examples of good ones are magic cubes, computer games, Etch-a-Sketch, travel bingo, magic slates, and snake puzzles. And don't forget books, including coloring books with crayon box secured to them (use large crayons that cannot easily get lost), dot-to-dot pictures, and crossword puzzle books. Keep toys for the car in a "car suitcase" kept near the door so they are ready to take along at a moment's notice.

Car activities that involve all riders include:

Group singing (rounds are excellent for older children)

Storytelling (a made-up story by one person or a group story where one person tells part and then passes it on to another)

Listening to tapes or the radio

Identifying things outside: "Let's find an oak tree"

Counting different objects such as 18-wheel trucks, flagpoles, cows, farms, or Christmas decorations

"I Spy" ("I spy something white that looks like cotton"—answer: clouds)

Rhyming things seen out the window

Twenty Questions

I Packed My Grandmother's Trunk

Identifying different signs

While driving your child home from school, you might want to ask how the day went. If you ask a general question, you will get a one-word answer—usually "Fine" or "Nothing." Try

1. What was the best/worst/most exciting thing that happened to you today?
2. What made you feel good/bad today?
3. What games did you play today?
4. Whom did you eat lunch with?
5. Tell me a story about something you did today.

FOOD IN THE CAR

If you are picking children up from school and dinner won't be served for several hours, a snack might be appropriate. Avoid any food that can get the car or children messy and do not bring salty food because they will want to stop for a drink. Fresh fruits or vegetables are easy and healthful snacks suitable for the car. Have individual (and identical) snacks for each child to avoid arguments. Keep a good trash receptacle in the car and disposable towels in the glove compartment.

12

Quality Time with Children

Most working parents cannot spend as much time with their children as they would like. However, the sheer amount of time you spend with your children is not as important as the quality of that time. The few minutes you spend with your child discussing the events of the day can be far more intimate and rewarding for both of you than an entire evening spent watching TV together. While it is important for the working mother to find and make time to be with her children, it is probably still more important for her to find and make *quality* time, and to make use of it when it appears spontaneously.

Commitment to this time is as important as the amount of it. Having breakfast at a favorite restaurant with your child once a week can be just as important as daily interactions. A lot has been written about quality time. Generally, I think of quality time as

> Any activity where you can show your child that you are interested in him, care about him, and love him
>
> Active participation and involvement by both children and parents
>
> Any activity that draws the family closer together
>
> Making (or strengthening) a connection of some kind between children and parents
>
> Children and parents all enjoying the activity and each other's company
>
> Any activity which helps foster in your child a sense of self-worth as a family member and as a member of society
>
> A feeling of happiness and satisfaction shared by all

Spend time with your children because you want to, **not** because you "owe it to them" or because you would feel guilty if you didn't. Children recognize guilt easily and will learn to use your guilt to their own advantage. "Guilt time" rarely turns into quality time.

The amount of time needed by children varies greatly, as does the kind of situations where they need love and support. All children need some of your time and attention, however. If it is difficult for you to give your time spontaneously, plan for it in advance. Schedule times for outings, games, family discussions, and other specific activites. Once you have scheduled an activity, do not cancel or postpone it unless you absolutely have to. These times are very important to your children, and if you take your commitments to them seriously they will feel that you love them and take them seriously.

Try to spend at least some quality time (talking, cuddling, playing games, working together on a project or hobby, just relaxing together) with your children each day. This will not actually be possible every day, but it will be most of the time. Children need parents at some times more than others. Be alert for times when your child needs you (during illness or severe disappointment, after a fight with another child) and try to give him the attention he needs. Children will not always let you know directly when they need you the most, so pay attention to the signs. Each child has his own signals, but some common ones are when the child is

Unusually quiet
Crying
Short-tempered
Not eating
Not participating in fun activities
Avoiding friends
Behaving strangely or differently

Learn to recognize your child's signals and respond positively and appropriately. As always, keep a sense of balance; don't spoil your child or make him or her too dependent on you. Quality time should be directed at assisting your child's mental and emotional growth, as well as a sense of well-being.

Erik Erickson's theory of developmental tasks specifies the general needs of children according to age.

AGE	THINGS TO DO OR PROVIDE FOR YOUR CHILD
Birth–12 months	Consistent care Body contact Affection Feed, hold, and sing to your baby often.
1–3 years	Establish routines and rituals. Try to be home around the same time each day. If a routine is broken, explain why. Maintain a safe home environment. Allow your child the opportunity to explore the world. Spend at least one-half hour a day in active play or interaction with your toddler; your husband should do the same. Toddler cries easily but cheers up even faster. Don't worry if he cries when you leave.
3–6 years	Allow your child to do things for himself. Your child will like to imitate his parents and join in their activities. Let him. Set realistic limits and expectations. Share your work experience with your child.
6–12 years	Share daily activities with your child. Praise your child for work accomplished.

Do not expect too much.

Do not pressure your child to succeed.

Attend important social and school events such as class plays and conferences.

Your child is learning the rules of life, which should be discussed and reinforced at home.

12 years and up   Your child will seek independence but still needs his parents in crises and for listening to his ideas and thoughts. Be available.

Plan time to be together.

Know your child's nonverbal clues and messages and respond appropriately.

Give each child individual attention away from his siblings.

Use days off to catch up on time with kids you didn't have during workdays. Find out from your children what they would like to do with you alone and with you and your husband together. Or give them several alternatives and let them select. As much as possible, try to do things that everyone involved (including parents) wants to do. If more than one child is involved in a decision, compromises may be necessary. A special occasion does not result in quality time unless you are willing to put your energy, attention, and caring into it (and into your children during the activity). During a one-on-one activity with your child, do not allow interruptions or distractions. Take the phone off the hook if necessary and don't compete with the TV or radio. Concentrate your complete attention on your child and the activity you are sharing. Don't try to do something else (knitting, ironing, washing dishes) at the same time. Also, try not to be planning or thinking about other things. Your child deserves your complete attention.

Try to determine the special needs of each of your children. When you are with each child, try to meet those particular needs first and foremost. If you cannot meet a child's request immediately, make sure your child sees you put it on your calendar (or on a priority list) so that he or she knows it is important to you and will get done. If you plan the activity, of course, be sure to actually do it. Honesty and clear, open communication are crucial for making the time spent with your children rewarding.

If you can afford to hire outside help to do routine jobs (cleaning, cooking, laundry), you may be able to create more uninterrupted time with your kids (see Chapter 4, "Choosing Child Care," and Chapter 5, "Hiring Outside Help"). If you do hire outside help for this reason, be sure you take advantage of it and actually do spend more time with your children.

There are only so many hours in a day. Many parents find that they simply must cut back somewhere to spend the kind of time they want or need to with their children. This sometimes means limiting social engagements, working part-time instead of full-time, or getting less sleep. (Sometimes we get more sleep than we need simply out of habit.) Decide what has to go and what you can reasonably afford to drop. You may find that despite all your efforts, you simply cannot spend as much time with your children as you would like. If this is the case, don't be angry with yourself. Instead, try to make the time that is available as productive and rewarding as possible. Remember, sometimes just being there is the important thing.

CREATING QUALITY TIME

Ordinary activities and chores (cooking, walking the dog, gardening, shopping) are opportunities for teaching as well as open communication with your children. Try to use these activities as times to be close to your children and share things with them.

Mealtimes are also great opportunities to spend quality time together, though they are frequently not used to their full potential. Instead of watching TV during dinner or eating in silence, discuss a common interest or problem. Let every family member have his or her say, and be sure to listen carefully. Or encourage each family member to discuss an important event that occurred during the day. A good question for young kids is "What was the very best thing that happened to you today?" or "What was the worst thing about your day?" The answer can provide you with insight into your child's feelings as well as the opportunity for family communication.

Use TV selectively. Do not use it as a babysitter or as a distraction or just to pass the time, either for yourself or your children. However, if TV is used carefully and selectively, watching a special or educational program with your children can become quality time.

Going places together creates great opportunities for quality time. Errands, visiting, sightseeing, or even chauffeuring can be made into special activities if communication is open and honest. Driving in a car alone with a child provides an excellent opportunity for direct one-to-one communication.

Make appointments with your children to have lunch, supper, or breakfast together away from home. This can be as simple as toast and milk at a coffee shop before work. Put this time on your calendar.

Bedtime is a favorite hour to establish rituals of quality time. Reading, singing, or just talking are favorite activities of many families. This is a good time for private discussions of the past day's activities or plans for the next day. This is the one time that is universally very important to children.

With a little ingenuity, any day can be made into a special occasion—the birthday of a pet, or an unbirthday; the planting of a tree; the first green bud of spring; the first snowfall; the first spring day; the solstice or equinox.

Talk about past special days or activities you have shared with your children: "Do you remember when we . . . ?" This is excellent for mealtimes and bedtime.

Just because you have scheduled an hour to be with your children does not mean your children will have the same idea when that time rolls around, even if they have been looking forward to it. Sometimes they will change their minds at the last minute. A more attractive activity may have turned up or they may just be tired or in bad moods. Be flexible and avoid becoming too frustrated or angry when the hour has been wasted on sibling fighting, going to the bathroom, getting a snack, or just whining.

Your husband should spend his share of quality time with the kids, too. Often while one of you is with the children, the other can accomplish a few chores or just relax.

Short periods of time spent with children may be more fun and rewarding than longer periods. Young children do not have a very long attention span and four or five ten-minute periods may be more beneficial (and easier to handle) than a full hour without a break.

Try to avoid favoritism in spending time with each of your children, and remember that time in which the whole family is together is as important as time alone with each individual child. Be sure to schedule this family time into your week.

Quality time should be viewed as cumulative. Look at the time you have spent with your children over the course of a week rather than at the end of each day. Some hectic days we may give children zero time, while other days (weekends and vacations, especially) we make up for it. Even mothers who are not employed and stay home have terrible days that result in no quality time with kids. Don't feel guilty if you have such days yourself.

Children usually respond better and are generally happier and more cooperative when they are well rested and well fed. Try to schedule time with your children accordingly. The hour right after dinner is ideal for many families. Plan activities that are appropriate for the time and for the child's mood and energy level. For instance, if it is near bedtime, don't try to teach your child magic tricks; he will undoubtedly get frustrated and angry as well as overstimulated. Tell him a story or do some other relaxing activity instead. If your schedule is such that you can only be with your child at difficult times of the day (before meals or late in the evening), try to be flexible and understanding. Time spent with children does not have to be perfect, or scheduled for the same time every day. (Rarely is it either one.)

Good organization and household management are the keys to having enough time for children. See Chapter 2, "Household Management," page 36. Important times in a child's day are before and after breakfast, before and after dinner, and around bedtime, and a working mother can usually be with her children at least some of these times.

Looking at family photos and movies always creates quality time. Kids love to see pictures of themselves and to follow the story of the family. Find hobbies that you and your children can work on together. Be willing to help your children with their schoolwork. If you are attentive and giving and show that you care, even this chore can become quality time. Cuddling, lying around together, listening to music, or some other quiet activity can be as rewarding as a planned outing.

Creating family traditions such as a family walk or weekly trip to an ice cream parlor results in long-term fond memories. Building or creating something together gives children a feeling of accomplishment and pride. Sharing in a creative endeavor can be educational as well as fun. Get a large piece of canvas and paint a design on it together—as wild as can be. Frame it and put it up in the children's room or den. Learn a new skill together. For example, take skiing lessons together; if your child progresses faster than you do, great! Have your child teach you something new—needlepoint, new math, a fact learned at school. Establish a special family hug or cheer. When everyone is feeling good about each other, indulge in this preestablished tradition.

Relax rules once in a while and let your child stay up past bedtime. Show your children you are flexible. Do your children's chores once in a while without being asked, especially if they have had a busy and tiring week. This is usually truly appreciated and results in their being more conscientious about their chores in the future. Avoid favoritism here, although it is fine to do one child's chore one week and the other's the next.

Take turns giving each other back rubs and singing soothing songs. Bathtime can be quality time to spend with your young child. It's usually a relaxing time where attention is focused on one another. You can teach new things, play together with bath toys, or discuss important happenings of the day. (Washing hair may be a different story!)

Performing simple experiments and discovering new things together provide memorable moments. Something as simple as making hand shadows on the wall fascinates young children. These can progress in complexity as the child gets older.

Care for a pet together. Plant a flower or vegetable garden with your children and experience together the pride that results. Have children help you in all kinds of activities. Even if they don't do them perfectly, thank them and show your appreciation. Don't make corrections in front of the child without gently explaining why. Be sure not to ask your child to help with something he is incapable of doing (or learning); this will only frustrate him, and you.

Explaining or showing children how things work can be rewarding as well as educational. Sharing and teaching go together. Take a task like ironing, or cooking, or painting; show your child how it is done, and then do it together. The results may be sloppy or inadequate at first, but once the child picks it up he will feel proud at being able to do an adult job with you. This builds his self-esteem and self-sufficiency and is an example of high-quality time.

13

After Work

The time at home after work when the whole family comes together provides an important opportunity for quality time for the entire family.

ARRIVING HOME

From the moment you walk through the door until you sit down to dinner can be one of the most hectic periods of the day. The activities associated with this time vary, depending on whether you pick up your children on the way home from work or they are already home when you get there.

If you pick up your children, the driving time provides a smooth transition between school and home when you can discuss important happenings of the day.

If children are already home, you will need to establish convenient and satisfactory routines for yourself and your family. Sticking to these routines is important for family harmony and efficiency, for winding down, and possibly for your sanity.

The first fifteen minutes after arriving home are especially important. If children need you immediately, perhaps putting down your handbag and giving the kids twenty minutes of undivided attention is best. After that, you can unwind and pamper yourself.

If you need the first fifteen minutes for yourself, however, make that clear, and after walking through the door, go straight to your "place," wherever that may be. Children will understand this need eventually. Be willing to deal with emergencies or special problems as soon as you walk in. These will come up occasionally and you will need to be available.

As a compromise, you might fix a beverage for yourself and your spouse and fruit juice for the kids, and have the whole family sit and relax, all sharing in the conversation.

Other ideas for surviving the first moments at home are:

1. Get off the bus a few blocks away from home and enjoy a walk.
2. Get a tape deck in your car and learn to relax driving home.
3. Hire a babysitter to entertain kids for one hour after you get home. This allows you time to unwind and prepare dinner.
4. Hire someone (perhaps a teenager) to come to your home an hour before you arrive to start dinner and set the table.
5. Have children do their homework before dinner. This gives you a chance to have some quiet time and then, after dinner, the family can share time and activities together.

Dinnertime should be shared by the entire family. If possible, all members should assist in preparing, cooking, serving, and cleaning up afterward. See Chapter 14, "Meals," page 184, for further tips on dinner.

AFTER-DINNER AND EVENING ACTIVITIES

Reserve some time after dinner to spend with your children. This is one of the few times for working people to be with the family. Having coffee after dinner and watching TV with the family provides a comfortable, relaxing time together. Watch good programs the whole family can enjoy. The TV should be used with discretion, however. It should not be a mere distraction or a babysitter for the children. In general, TV should be discouraged except when there is something really worth watching.

Working together on chores and/or hobbies such as homework, sewing, painting, or reading are popular activities for the evening hours. This is a great time to review schoolwork and discuss future plans and activities as well as to practice piano, dancing, or gymnastics.

Families also participate in outside activities such as evening ball games, school plays, competitive games, church programs, and various other events. Parents should try to attend some of their children's activities in which case the dinner hour may have to be changed.

BEDTIME

Most children are usually ready to go to bed well before they are willing to. Bedtimes should be reasonable and meet children's needs. Crying, pleading, and begging to stay up longer should not influence the time they are put to bed. If children know that the times are fair, they will adhere to them most of the time.

It is all right to establish a separate bedtime for each child, provided they are different ages. Occasionally a younger child will protest that it isn't fair—but it is. Activities should wind down as bedtime approaches; it is difficult to change gears instantaneously. A warm bath has a calming effect as do cookies with warm milk or hot chocolate.

If more than one child goes to bed at the same time, they can be read a story together—or each parent can read to one child, alternating children each night. This gives each adult the chance to spend some time alone with each child, and vice versa. Although bedtime is an important time for parents to be with children, parents should not feel obliged to do this every night. A babysitter is quite capable of putting children to bed.

Bedtime rituals are especially important and comforting to

young children and should be maintained even by babysitters. Rituals can include all kinds of activities, such as reading, making up stories, talking together, hugging, kissing, saying prayers, and singing lullabys. Rubbing backs and singing are favorites of young children, and don't forget a good-night kiss.

Other routines, such as using the bathroom, drinking a cup of juice, and brushing teeth are equally important to children. Night hygiene—brushing and flossing teeth, using the toilet, and washing hands and face—should be established in children at a very young age, ideally around two or three. A small night light should be left on in each child's room to enable them to see if they wake up and to allow you or the babysitter to see when checking on them.

Some parents have dinner after the children go to bed. This gives them time to be with the children before bedtime and time to be alone together after the children are asleep. If you choose this option, bedtime should not be rushed because of it. If children go to bed early, around 7:00 or 8:00 P.M., parents have a good part of the evening to talk, relax, or accomplish their work. It also ensures that children get enough rest. Early bedtime may be a habit you want to establish early in a child's life so that it will be more readily accepted as the child gets older.

14

Meals

GENERAL INFORMATION

A balanced diet occurs over time. No one single meal or day's meals constitutes a good or bad diet. To see if you are serving balanced meals, look at what you serve over the course of a week or two; then make adjustments as necessary. Establish good nutritional habits (such as discouraging lots of sweets and other empty calories) from the time your children are infants.

If you want your children to eat a balanced diet, you must eat a balanced diet yourself. Children will do what you do, not what you say to do. Do not serve your children foods that are "good" for them if you will not eat them yourself. Double standards never work.

Simplify meals, both in preparation and cooking. Remember, you don't need a three-course hot dinner every day. Keep your pantry well stocked, especially with staples.

The four basic food groups are guides to good nutrition. Current daily recommendations include:

RECOMMENDED DAILY INTAKE

Milk group including milk, cheese, ice cream, or other products made with whole or skimmed milk — 2 servings for adults, 4 servings for teenagers, 3 servings for children

Meat group including beef, veal, lamb, pork, poultry, — 2 servings

fish, eggs, dry beans or
peas, nuts, peanut butter,
soy extenders

Vegetables and fruits—   4 servings
dark green, leafy, or orange
vegetables and fruit recommended 3 or 4 times weekly
for vitamin A; citrus fruit
recommended daily for vitamin C

Breads, pasta, and ce-   4 servings
reals—whole grain, fortified,
or enriched grain products

Efforts should be made to include these foods in your children's
daily diet. Buy convenience foods with discretion. Some convenience foods are satisfactory from a nutritional standpoint and do
save time. Read the package information clearly and avoid foods
with large quantities of added sugar.

Organize your kitchen well. Group similar items together and
make sure utensils are easy to find and reach, especially if your
children are old enough to prepare some of their own meals. Be
sure everything is labeled, including all bottles.

Have the right equipment for easy cooking, including sharp
knives, different size casserole dishes, etc. (see Chapter 2, "Appliances," page 41, for more information). Keep an easy-to-use
recipes file.

Invest in some cookbooks of easy, fast recipes. Preparation and
cooking time should be included in each recipe.

Although many families are not having a "family meal" together as often as they once did, a significant number of families still
do get together for a meal several times a week. To take greater
advantage of these shared eating experiences, share the work of
mealtimes with the family. The entire job of a meal can be rotat-
ed among family members, or each person can assume a specific
job according to ability. The various jobs of a meal include:

Last-minute shopping

Food preparation—including grating, dicing, cutting, mixing, and everything else before cooking (can be subdivided into courses—salad, main dish, dessert)

Cooking

Setting table

Serving

Clearing table

Washing dishes

Drying dishes

Putting away dishes

Sweeping floor

Taking out garbage

Assign duties to members of the family if no one volunteers. Post assignments so all can see and remember their duties.

There are dozens of books concerning nutrition, diets, cooking, and storing foods. Invest in ones consistent with your family's values and beliefs about food. A great deal of time and effort are wasted on jumping on the bandwagon of each new food fad.

For health and a minimum of confusion and interruption, children should go to the bathroom and wash their hands before they sit down to meals. Policies for table behavior should be discussed and decided upon as a family unit.

1. Does everyone have to show up at the table at the same time?

2. May TV, radio, and telephone be used during mealtime?

3. How much of the food on their plates do the children have to eat?

4. What are the talking rules? Does everyone get a turn, or can anyone talk who wants to? Can separate conversations be occurring at the same time or will there be a single family discussion during meals?

5. When can anyone leave the table, and for what reasons?

6. Are the rules the same for all three meals, or do they differ from meal to meal? There is nothing wrong with different rules for different meals, or for weekends and weekdays.

7. Under what circumstances can the rules be changed or temporarily suspended? Remember that as schedules become more varied, rules will have to be manipulated to ease the tension of the "overcommitted calendar." So be flexible while attempting to impose some order on the family meal.

MEAL PLANNING

The following items are intended primarily for dinners, but apply equally well to lunches and brunches.

Plan menus in advance for at least one week at a time. Determine the approximate time needed to prepare each meal and be sure it fits into your family's schedule. This can be done at a family conference so that everyone can make suggestions and agree to (or at least be aware of) the final menu.

After the week's menu has been decided on, locate (or write up if necessary) the appropriate recipes. Make a shopping list of needed items. Include any general items that you are running low on. List the foods by groups, depending on their location in the store. Note which dishes or meals can (or need to) be prepared in advance. Marinating meats, soaking beans, and defrosting need to be done the night or morning before.

In families where schedules change and family members arrive home at different times, it might be advantageous to make up "general-idea" menus for a week without attaching specific dates or times to each meal. If recipes have specific preparation and cooking times detailed, whoever arrives home first can begin a meal that can be prepared and cooked within the allotted time span. This works well with families with teenagers. You might post a note on the message center that details what the first one home should do. For example:

FIRST ONE HOME, BUT
NOT BEFORE 5:00 P.M.

1. Turn on oven to 325°.
2. Put chicken from refrigerator in baking pan sitting on counter.
3. Sprinkle with paprika on counter. Put pan in oven.
4. Set timer for 1 hour.
5. Turn oven off in 1 hour and remove chicken from oven. Cover with aluminum foil and leave on top of stove.
6. Set table.
7. That's it! Good job!
8. Call me at work if you have any questions.
9. I love you.

mom.

Make and post notes the night before; in the morning things may be too hectic and time may be too short to write out directions. Leave explicit directions, no matter how simple the task. Of course, the directions will depend on how experienced your family members are and what details you went over the night or morning before.

MEAL PREPARATION

Emergency ready-made meals should always be available in the house. For example, frozen pizzas are great to have when everyone has been delayed getting home and it's too late in the evening to start anything from scratch. One-dish meals are easy and popular. These can be nutritionally sound and can be prepared in advance. Leftovers can then be stored easily. Examples include tuna and hamburger casseroles, lasagna, and hearty soups. A large freezer is extremely helpful in storing cooked or ready-to-cook dishes for future use.

When cooking, try to cook for more than one meal at a time. It is probably easier to do this on a day off or over a weekend. Double or triple the recipes and freeze the leftovers for another day. This way you cook only half (or one-third) as often and can choose when to do your cooking; you won't have to cook when time is short. For many meals, you need simply to reheat and serve the food. Cooking and freezing in advance should be considered for all meals, including those for special occasions. Store leftovers in dishes that you can use to reheat and serve the food in order to eliminate unnecessary transfers of food and potwashing.

You might consider spending several hours (on a weekend, a day off, or late at night) cooking several different dishes at once. You may wish to do this at the same time each week—this way you only have to cook once a week.

In preparing food for the week's meals, consider cutting up onions, carrots, or other time-consuming ingredients all at once and storing them in the refrigerator or freezer. This allows young children to participate in meal preparation in the evening without the hassles of chopping or slicing.

When freezing an item, label it clearly with the description of the item and the date you stored it. Also keep a master list of the freezer contents. Freeze food in small containers so that you thaw and cook only as much food as your family can eat at one meal. It is a good idea to freeze some food in single-serving containers so that you can prepare a single meal when necessary. These single servings are also convenient if a sitter needs to serve a meal to your children. If your child is old enough, he can heat up and serve his own meal.

BREAKFAST

The morning is one of the most hectic times of the day. Take this into account when planning and cooking breakfast. A simple breakfast can be as nutritious as a complex, hot, three-course meal.

If possible, prepare for breakfast the night before; at least, set the table. Make juice the night before, if frozen, and store it in the refrigerator. Cereal can be put in individual bowls, set on the table, and covered with plastic wrap.

Encourage children to prepare their own breakfast. For young children, put juice and milk in small individual pitchers, empty baby-food jars, or plastic measuring cups. The children can handle these alone with little risk of spilling them. Place them in a convenient spot in the refrigerator where children can reach them easily.

Some day-care centers and latchkey programs serve breakfast. Usually there is a small additional charge. Be sure the breakfasts are nutritious, low in sugar, and tasty enough that your child will eat them (there is no point in paying for meals your child will not eat). Be especially careful about the sugar issue as some institutional breakfasts are very heavy on the sugar.

Quick, easy, and nutritious breakfast foods include:

1. Cold cereals. Some of these (shredded wheat, Familia, Grape-Nuts) are quite nutritious with milk, and they are tasty. A surprisingly large number of packaged cereals are largely sugar, however—including corn flakes and puffed wheat, most commercial granola, and many of the "health" and high-vitamin cereals. Read the nutritional information and the list of ingredients carefully. If sugar is one of the first two or three ingredients, steer clear. (Dextrose and glucose are two types of sugar; be on the lookout for these ingredients too.)

2. Whole fruits are very easy to serve. Teach children how to peel them as soon as they are old enough.

3. Peanut butter sandwiches are a favorite of kids for all meals. Peanut butter on toast, English muffins, or bagels is delicious and healthful.

4. Yogurt with dry cereal on top is a relatively new winner.

5. Pancake sandwiches with jam in the middle eliminate the mess of syrup.

6. Muffins with melted cheese (Cheddar, American, Swiss, or Muenster) are excellent. A toaster oven, broiler, or microwave helps in fast cooking.

7. Combine the last bits of different breakfast cereals in one bowl for your own creative cereal, or sprinkle this mixture on plain yogurt.

8. Granola bars and milk are yummy.

9. Bagels with cream cheese, hard cheese, butter, or jelly can be prepared, wrapped, and stored in the refrigerator the night before.

10. Milk shakes containing milk, eggs, bananas, melon, vanilla, or other ingredients are quick, easy, and nutritious. A blender or similar appliance is a necessity in combining ingredients.

11. Hard cheese and crackers are favorites.

12. French toast can be made the night before, wrapped in foil, and refrigerated. In the morning, reheat in the same foil.

13. A variety of nutritious cookies containing nuts, wheat germ, oatmeal, and peanut butter can be baked. Two or three of these cookies, a piece of fruit, and a glass of milk can make a breakfast, and you should have few problems in getting kids to eat it. Be sure to go very low on the sugar or honey and high on the other ingredients.

BREAKFAST IN THE CAR

All working mothers at one time or another have to feed their children en route to work. No matter how well we plan, sometimes it's just too late to prepare or eat breakfast at home. Some simple foods for breakfast on wheels are:

Banana, bread, and butter (toast makes crumbs)

Apple, bread, and butter (no peel to deal with)

Dry cereal, either in individual boxes or in paper cups

Bagel, butter, and/or cream cheese or hard cheese

Nutritious cookies

Granola bars

Sometimes the drive-through window at a doughnut shop is the only alternative. This is okay once in a while. Remember, a nutritious diet occurs over time so don't feel guilty about occasional junk food. See Chapter 11, page 161, for hints on food in the car.

LUNCH

Although lunches are frequently eaten at home, this section deals with those eaten away from home—at work, school, or the day-care center. Plan lunches for a week at a time and ask for suggestions from those who will eat them. Consider the dinner menu in planning, as well as nutrition and variety.

Use leftovers for lunch. For those who carry brown bags or lunch boxes, pack nonperishable items such as cookies, chips, or fruit the night before. Thermos bottles for hot food should be heated before use by filling them with boiling water. Food stays hot longer this way.

Although adults usually like to vary their lunches, children will often be satisfied with the same sandwich day after day. Be sure to inform the babysitter, teacher, or your child if a lunch must be refrigerated.

If you pack lunches for your children, be sure you pack enough, and that the lunches are nutritious. Lunch is meant to be eaten, not thrown away. Prepare something your child likes and will eat at least some of. Check school and day-care policies regarding throwing food away. Make sure an empty lunch box is not the result of a thrown-away lunch.

If you want variety in a packaged lunch, consider packing the same type of meal you would serve at home. There are many useful containers for safely carrying casseroles, soups, and sauces. There are even small ones made especially for condiments.

Guard against spoilage. (This is not as big a problem now that there are so many handy insulated containers available.) Many spoiled foods do not smell bad and therefore smell does not necessarily determine spoilage.

If children buy their lunch or milk, be sure they have money or lunch tickets and double-check before they leave for school. Secure money or ticket in a safe place where the child will not lose it, such as in a small purse tucked in a bookbag. If your child would rather bring lunch than buy it at school, pack it willingly. School cafeterias are not known for tasty food, and if you prepare a lunch you know your child will eat at least some of it.

Usually babysitters will feed babies. Be sure to leave detailed instructions with a supply of food with the sitter or at the day-care center. A child with special food needs or problems must be handled on an individual basis. Inform the school or center; most institutions are set up to handle large numbers of people and they must be prodded to provide for special cases. Be sure to make the effort if individual routines or procedures need to be followed for your child, as the school or center will not do it otherwise.

DINNER

In many households, dinner is the one meal the family eats together and is therefore a fine opportunity for quality time. See Chapter 12, page 166, for further hints in this area.

COOKING WITH KIDS

Cooking together can be a very positive experience for you and your children. Not only does it allow for time together, it teaches important life skills while accomplishing an essential task. The learning that occurs during cooking involves varied skills, including hand coordination and manipulation, reading, following written and verbal directions, counting, measuring, and distinguishing tastes. Cooking is an extremely important and useful skill for your child to have now and as an adult.

Teach kids to cook for themselves and for the family at an early age. This makes them self-reliant and saves you lots of time and trouble. A child who can cook can be left alone at home for a whole day if necessary.

Cooking can involve the entire family, including children of all ages. It can be an intimate and rewarding experience that everyone can share. Cooking with your children (and having your children cook with one another) teaches cooperation and sharing. Each child can be given a useful job to accomplish (within his ability). Even three-year-olds can fetch or pour or stir ingredients. Most kids find cooking fun once they get the hang of it. Their ability to cook increases their self-esteem; many will feel proud of this skill and some will even ask for the privilege of cooking.

TEACHING YOUR CHILDREN TO COOK

You can teach each child to cook individually or teach them cooking skills together. At first, young children can be trained to help adults cook. Then they can be taught to work with one another. Next, each child can be taught to cook meals on his or her own. No special equipment is needed for teaching a child to cook. The simpler the recipe and the equipment, the better, at least at first. Choose times convenient for all, and allow ample time for detailed explanation, mistakes, and slow movement. You should not introduce new cooking skills to children when you are under time pressure. Go slowly and don't expect too much too quickly.

Start with simple recipes that can be eaten that day. A child's favorite food is a good place to begin. Be sure all ingredients are available. Lacking an important ingredient can cause disappointment, tears, and possibly even disaster; until your child is adept at cooking, he or she will not know how to vary a recipe or substitute an ingredient.

Before your kids begin to cook, read through the recipe with them carefully and make sure they understand it thoroughly. Younger kids love to pour and mix many ingredients. Older children can actually do the food preparation—cutting, slicing, separating eggs, etc.

Introduce the use of small kitchen appliances to children under careful supervision. Go over safety rules. Make sure children understand clearly the following precautions:

1. Tie back long hair.
2. Wash hands before beginning.
3. Always turn pot handles in toward the stove to avoid bumping them.
4. When using a knife, always cut with the sharp edge facing away from your hand. Put food firmly on the cutting board and hold it down with curled-up fingers. Never cut food while holding it in your fingers.
5. Turn off the oven or the burner right after you have finished using it. Double-check that all burners and the oven are turned off when you have finished cooking.
6. Turn off electrical appliances and pull out their plugs as soon as you have finished with them. Pull plugs out of the wall socket before removing the electrical elements from the appliances.
7. Use pot holders for any hot pots or dishes. If you are not sure whether something is hot or not, use a pot holder to be safe.
8. Don't touch an electrical appliance or cord with wet hands or with a wet pot holder.
9. Pour hot liquids away from you to avoid steam burns.
10. Read labels to make sure you have what you want. Do not trust the appearance of an ingredient; some substances (for example, sugar and salt; cornmeal and Parmesan cheese) look alike.
11. Clean up spills immediately to avoid slipping on them.
12. Be sure to shut the refrigerator and freezer doors tightly.
13. If an oven or burner on a gas stove fails to light, turn it off and leave it off.
14. If grease catches fire, smother it with a lid or by pouring baking soda or salt on it. Do not use water.
15. Keep boxes, towels, pot holders, and all other cloth and paper items away from burners.

16. If food smells funny, don't use it. Check with an adult, or use something else.
17. Don't use food from a can that bulges.
18. Go over fire precautions with your child. Explain what to do in case of fire.
19. Use a long-handled wooden spoon or a metal spoon with a wooden or plastic handle when stirring a hot mixture on the stove. Never leave a spoon in the pot. If a spoon falls in, retrieve it with tongs, not with your fingers.
20. Never put metal or aluminum foil in a microwave oven.

Supervise your child the first several times he or she cooks. Give generous praise for effort and accomplishments.

Allow children to prepare meals or parts of meals even if the results do not look or taste as good as yours. With practice, their meals will improve and may become as good as or better than yours.

As your child grows older, you can teach more complicated tasks and more complex recipes. (The next step is cooking without recipes!) There are many cookbooks for beginners. Two fairly easy ones are:

The Children's Cookbook, A Beginner's Guide to Cooking. Favorite Recipes Press/Nashville, P.O. Box 77, Nashville, Tennessee 37202

Kim's Cookbook for Young People. Red Farm Studio, Pawtucket, Rhode Island 02860

15

Traveling Moms

More and more women have jobs that require trips away from their homes and families. Although men have traditionally left home for several days for business purposes, the traveling mother faces new and additional challenges. When considering a job that requires traveling, discuss the pros and cons with your family. If they feel part of the decision-making process, they will more easily accept your being away. Of course, if your family is adamant about your not traveling, you should not take the job. Some jobs may strain family relations a bit; no job should undermine them.

Set limits on your traveling if possible. For example, you might agree to a maximum of two three-day trips per month. Stick to your limits. Your family can adjust easier if they know in advance how much time you will be away.

When away, you should not give up all responsibilities to the adult left at home. You are still a parent, even when traveling, and you must keep in touch and participate in family decisions—by long distance, if need be. Use the telephone to keep in touch. Call your spouse and children daily. Learn about the children's day over the phone. The cost of the long-distance call should be part of your business expenses. Don't forget to give your family your hotel room number and phone numbers where you can be reached in case of emergency.

Be very specific about the time you will be home. If you are not sure, tell them the very latest time you will return. Don't promise to be home at a certain time and then have to extend it. It's better to surprise the family by an early arrival than to disappoint them with a later one.

Maintain a traveling schedule that allows you time at home between trips. This enables you to keep the household running smoothly and perhaps even to catch your breath. Try to be home on weekends and on important days such as birthdays, school plays, and recitals. Try to avoid or postpone trips that interfere with special family, school, or church events.

Write a postcard or letter to your children before you leave or while traveling, and drop it in the mail as soon as you arrive at your destination so that your child will get it before you return home, even if you are only gone a couple of days. Mail a separate letter or card for each child; children love to get their own mail.

Establish exciting rituals for when you return home. Some families go out to dinner the night the traveling parent returns —or the traveler might put all the children to bed. Bringing children gifts is a mixed blessing. Sometimes you are extremely busy from the beginning of the trip to the end and have no time to purchase gifts. If you start buying items at airports, you will find that they are costly and that selection is poor. Children will begin to expect a present each time you are away and will be disappointed if they don't receive one. If you like to buy presents, don't do it consistently. Kids should not expect a present for each business trip. (An alternative is to buy a gift while still at home and pack it in your suitcase. You then have a useful gift bought at a reasonable price.)

Let teachers know that you will be away and for how long so that in case your child acts out or becomes melancholy, the teacher will understand the reason.

Tell your children where you will be going. For example, if you are going to New York City, talk about the city and show pictures of it if you can. Go to the library and borrow a book about New York so that your family can share your trip with you vicariously. Buy a large map or puzzle map of the United States (or, if need be, the world) and point out the places you will be visiting. Use this opportunity as a geography lesson as well as a means of helping your child become involved in your trip.

Make tape recordings for your children that they can play while you are away. Tape a storybook for them and they can listen to it before going to bed. This maintains a real link with your children while you are away. Be sure to say "I love and miss you very much" at the end of the tape. If you are visiting a new city that the family has never been to, take photographs to share with them or buy post cards or books with pictures of interesting sites.

If you find that your children were upset while you were away, go over the arrangements you made for them and be sure their needs were being met. In addition, talk to the entire family and try to obtain realistic feelings from them regarding your travel. If your spouse is angry about being left alone, this may be communicated to the children and create all kinds of behavior problems. Let everyone express feelings, concerns, and worries. You may have to make some adjustments in your schedule or arrangements but don't give up on traveling too quickly. Once your family knows you are willing to stay home at the first sign of tears, you will never be free. Work out problems and try new solutions. Be creative and do what you can to improve child-care arrangements. If your family realizes that travel is a part of your life— and at the same time that this doesn't decrease their importance to you—then this usually works out.

On your return from a trip, be sure to spend the first few hours with your family, if at all possible. This will help show them how much they mean to you. If you are away for more than two or three days, you may want to hire a live-in housekeeper for that time. These helpers can be located through babysitting agencies. (Also see Chapters 4 and 5.) Be sure to state any specific requirements, such as if the children must be driven to an activity. Arrange to have additional help come in to clean or prepare meals.

Relatives may be willing to spend some time with your family in your absence. The children may enjoy staying with their grandparents, other relatives, or friends while you are gone. This can be a mini-vacation for them if it doesn't happen too frequently.

If possible, arrange a combination business trip and family vacation. This can be fun for everyone—and your trip can still be considered a tax deduction!

All home and child-care arrangements should be made prior to your business trip. Prepare a checklist with explicit directions similar to the sample below.

CHECKLIST WHILE MOM IS AWAY

MOM'S ITINERARY
Destination _____

Depart: Date: _____

         Time: _____ Arrival: _____

         Airline & Flight # _____

Travel to Airport _____

Return: Date: _____

         Time: _____ Arrival: _____

         Airline & Flight # _____

Hotel: Name _____

      Phone _____

Other Phone Numbers: _____

Schedule:

HOME SCHEDULE:
Meals:

    Dates: _____   _____   _____

    Breakfast:

    Lunch:

    Dinner:

BABYSITTING ARRANGEMENTS:
  Before school:

  After school:

  Nights:

Special activities:
  Dates: _____   _____   _____

  Other:

16

Single Mothers

All the hints in this book apply to single-parent families as well as two-parent households. This chapter, however, addresses some special problems of the home with a working mother and no father/husband.

When you become a single parent, either through death or divorce, take things slowly. Do not make any major changes immediately. If possible, put off decisions until the acute trauma of the event has passed. Thoughts are more rational and decisions wiser over time.

Many times children blame themselves for the death of a parent or for a divorce. All children wish a parent bad things sometimes and they may believe it was through their wishes that the event occurred. Be sure that your children know they were not responsible for the divorce or death in any way. Reassuring children that you will not desert them is important at this time, as children grow concerned that their remaining parent may leave them also.

Family support can assist the single-parent family in coping with the many challenges, frustrations, and misgivings that may arise. This support can come from your immediate family, an extended family, other single-parent families, friends, church groups, or professionally established support groups. Be open with your children about changes that may occur within the family due to your new status. A mother who never worked may have to find a job, finances may be tighter, vacations may be eliminated. One of the major single-family organizations is Parents Without Partners (PWP). Their address is Suite 1000, 7910 Woodmont Avenue, Washington, D.C. 20014. They can provide the names of local support and information groups and services.

If divorced, decide with your ex-spouse on communication patterns and discipline regarding the children. Don't let the children play one parent against the other. This is not healthy for the children or the parents. The father of your child is still the father. He should provide support and be an active participant in your child's upbringing. If possible, attempt to reconcile the anger of the divorce. Encourage him to share in some of the child-care responsibilities, even if he seems reluctant.

Look for groups that can offer male role models for young children. Some nursery schools have male teachers, and public schools frequently have male faculty. See the principal and request these teachers (if they have good reputations) for your children. If possible, talk with potential teachers to see if they provide the kind of models you want for your children. Scouts, Big Brother programs, Boys' Clubs, and athletic activities also all provide male role models. Be selective and don't overburden your children with too many different activities and commitments. Junior Achievement and 4-H provide girls with male role models.

Continue to share activities with married friends and their families. They can provide male role models for your child and a stabilizing influence for your family. Don't cut off contact with your married friends just because your marital status has changed. Having your children talk to other children of divorced parents sometimes helps in answering the questions that they cannot ask you for one reason or another. Be selective in the choice of children—you want someone who has adjusted to the situation.

Make sure you spend some quality time with your child every day, even if it is only fifteen minutes. Tell him that this is his time and do something that is enjoyable for both of you. Let your child select the activity, if possible. This interlude is especially important in single-parent families. (See Chapter 12, "Quality Time with Children," page 162, for more information.)

Let the child's teacher or babysitter know when you become

a single parent. This knowledge assists the teacher in understanding a child whose behavior may change due to a changed home situation. Teachers are usually very supportive if they understand the cause of a behavior change.

You cannot be supermom, and things cannot be exactly as they were when you were a two-parent family. Admit this to yourself (and to your children) and decide what the new priorities are. Try to be realistic; this saves pain and trouble later. You will simply not have as much time as you did before, and money and patience may be shorter, too. Do not promise your child something you cannot deliver, especially if it is something you could or did provide before.

Sometimes joining households with another single-parent family makes life easier. Although this arrangement may have its problems, people who have found the right family find it easier and more rewarding for all concerned.

Encourage children who can write to record their feelings about a divorce or death. This may help them to clarify their own thoughts. Create new traditions for your smaller family. Replace old family rituals and "good times" with new traditions and activities.

Never talk negatively about the child's other parent to the child. Maintain routine disciplinary standards. Don't use your children as a substitute for your spouse. Although you should be honest with them, don't overburden them with worries and concerns over which they have no control. Continue to allow them to live their own lives.

Don't overindulge children with extravagant presents or activities and don't be manipulated by them. Don't dote on your children or smother them with attention or affection. This is not fair or nurturing for them. New single parents may need to be especially mindful of this.

Allow children to be a part of decision-making when questions arise that affect them. They will then accept the decisions more readily.

If you are looking for a job, try to look for one close to your home. Spending less time commuting allows you to spend more time with the children (and saves travel expenses). Discrimination against single parents continues to exist in jobs and rental housing. Be on guard and report any overt discriminatory practices.

Although being a single parent is difficult in many ways, there are some advantages to bringing up children alone. Children are often treated more as equals, and the family unit tends to be more democratic. One standard of behavior and discipline can be maintained fairly easily. Children become more independent and self-reliant.

JOINT CUSTODY

A fairly new option following divorce, joint custody gives equal rights and responsibilities for the children to each parent. The children spend equal time with each parent, and this time can be divided any way the family decides. Under joint custody, each parent must want the children and be a responsible and competent caregiver.

Since many issues must be dealt with and decided upon, an impartial mediator is sometimes retained to work out the joint custody terms. Older children may be included in the negotiations for these terms. The final agreement should clearly be in the children's best interests.

This arrangement is not right for everyone, but for those who do manage to work out the co-parenting details, it can create a satisfactory and rewarding modified family unit in which children receive the benefit of having both parents, and both parents share the responsibilities and rewards of raising their children.

17

Teenagers

Although many child-care problems end when children become teenagers, others develop at that time. Many parents feel that teenagers take more of their time and attention than younger children do.

Quality time should be given to teenagers with as much concern and attention as it is given to small children. Teenagers often have difficulty confiding in adults, mainly because of difficulty in verbalizing their own feelings. Listening to them when they express a need to talk is extremely important. Always use positive communication techniques and try never to criticize or condemn. Give praise frequently—whenever it is deserved. Parents should review their own values and morals before questioning those of their teenagers.

Set household rules and stick to them. If you do not stick to them yourself, or fully expect your teenager to stick to them, be assured that he or she will not. Of course, rules should be fair and reasonable. Establish clear consequences for not sticking to the rules, and make sure your teenager understands them before the rules go into effect. Rules might cover behavior at home, household responsibilities, curfew, and other areas of concern. Teenagers are learning to take responsibility for themselves and for their actions, and rules and their fair enforcement become more important for them than perhaps for any other age group.

Do not try to instill guilt in your teenagers. Guilt may be imposed manipulatively and often leads to feelings of resentment and anger which can be quite harmful. One example of a guilt-producing statement is: "You spent all your money on that cheap-looking blouse after I worked so hard to earn it! You just don't care how hard I work to give you what you want." The teen probably does care very much about how hard her mother works, but liked the blouse and thought it was a worthwhile purchase.

Don't throw up to your teenagers that they cause you worry. This will not help and may make them feel resentful or guilty. You will probably not be able to keep from worrying, but except in severe cases it is best to keep your anxiety to yourself.

Mood swings are common among adolescents and can be quite unsettling to the family. Ignoring the "bad periods" is probably the best way to deal with them.

Adequate sleep is important for teens and should be provided for within the household routines. Teenagers like to stay up late but may take naps if encouraged. They almost always have a difficult time getting up in the morning. Adequate nutrition and exercise are very important. Since few teenagers eat right or care about nutrition, it is important to serve balanced meals at home.

Hobbies and school athletics should be encouraged by parents —within limits—but should not interfere with schoolwork. Teenagers frequently have a full schedule of school and extracurricular activities and may not be available for odd jobs and errands at your convenience. This may be a change from a few years earlier when your child had more time to help around the house.

Teenagers should have prearranged household assignments agreed upon at the family conference well in advance of the time they need to be done. Because of teenagers' busy schedules, flexibility in household job activities helps them in getting the job done. Prescheduled time with teenagers may be helpful in bridging communication gaps. If your teen does not want to spend time with you, keep asking and making the effort. Although teenagers do not usually want to spend time with their family, your showing a desire to be with your teen in spite of your busy schedule demonstrates how important he or she is to you. Then when the need arises, your teen will know you are available.

Peers are extremely important to teens and they try unceasingly to obtain status and acceptance from their peer group. This is normal behavior and parents should understand that peer influence will usually be stronger than their own.

If problems occur, call a family meeting and explain and discuss the problem. Make sure everyone agrees with the statement of the problem, then brainstorm all possible solutions and use the techniques described on page 25 to decide on the one solution with the most positives and the fewest negatives. Make sure everyone, including the teenager, understands what all the positives and negatives are. Compromise should be a key in finding solutions to teenagers' problems. In a dispute, no one should be considered a winner or loser.

Share information with your teen, but allow him to make certain decisions concerning himself for himself. Teens want to be independent and should be allowed to assume responsibility for their own behavior. If you are unhappy with something your teenager does (or doesn't do), a written contract may be worth a try. Although it seems stiff, cold, and contrived, it works a surprising amount of the time. The contract should state both how you would like your son or daughter to change and what reward will be given once that change has taken place. Needless to say, if you do not offer as reward something the teenager wants, such a contract will do little good. Both you and your teenager should sign and date the contract, and it is a good idea to keep it posted in a place where both signers will see it frequently. Be sure the contract specifies all conditions, exceptions, and qualifications. Here is an example.

I, _____, will stop using profanity in the house, at school, in church, and in all other places, beginning immediately, in exchange for use of the car every other Saturday night. The use of the car will start one week after use of profanity has ceased.

Signed:_____ Date:_____
Son or daughter

Signed:_____ Date:_____
Parent

Be sure that in signing a contract you do not violate any agreements or understanding you have (or your child has) with other members of the family. Most important of all, do not offer a reward you are not fully prepared to give.

Allowances should be given with no strings attached, but extra money can be given for jobs that you would ordinarily pay someone else to do. If your teenager wants to clean the house instead of a cleaning service, pay what you would pay the service.

18

Costs of Working

There are many obvious as well as hidden costs associated with having a job and working. These costs should be carefully calculated and evaluated if you are considering taking (or continuing) a job solely for financial reasons. The hidden costs may mount up. Costs include:

1. *Child care.* Day care or babysitting costs (including before- or after-school care) may be associated with your work.

2. *Housekeeping.* Many mothers get outside help for housekeeping tasks because they are working.

3. *Clothes.* Jobs may require a uniform or a specific type of clothing not usually worn every day. Even if you do not need a uniform, you may need to increase your wardrobe to be dressed appropriately for work.

4. *Transportation.* Your job may mean increases in gas and car maintenance expenses, costs of parking and/or public transportation.

5. *Household maintenance.* You may need to hire helpers to fix things around the house, mow the lawn, shovel snow, etc., because you do not have the time or energy to do it yourself.

6. *Food.* Lunches may be an additional expense if you eat out while at work. Usually there is an increased grocery bill since many working mothers rely heavily on expensive convenience foods. Families with working mothers also tend to eat in restaurants more often.

7. *Job-seeking expenses.* There may be costs in locating a job, especially if you go through an agency or must travel to locate a position.

8. *Taxes.* Withholding tax both at the federal and state levels will increase if you become a two-paycheck family.

9. *Socializing.* These expenses involve everything from having lunch or a drink with co-workers or hosting a party at your house for your office to a donation for a coffee fund or toward a retirement gift. Although you can resist some of these costs, you may feel you cannot avoid them altogether.

10. *Education.* Some jobs require additional education, workshops, or training; often these expenses are not assumed by the employer.

11. *Charitable contributions.* Some employers put pressure on their employees to give to particular charities. This is not fair, but it happens.

There are very few tax benefits in having a job, and very few expenses are tax deductible. Child-care expenses provide a tax credit if you have a child under fifteen years old and pay for child care in order to work or attend school. Twenty to 30 percent of child-care expenses can be used as a tax credit, depending on the amount of salary you receive and the number of children you have. There are limits to the number of deductions you can claim.

If you claim an in-house babysitter, you must pay social security if she earned more than $50 in any one quarter. (Further information on child care is currently in IRS booklet 503.)

If your job requires a special uniform that cannot be worn at other places, the cost of the uniforms is tax deductible. Keep receipts.

Travel expenses in finding a job are only deductible for the year you accept a new job. Travel to and from work and associated costs are not deductible. If your job requires travel after you reach the main location, such as going to a secondary location or office for a short time and then returning to the main office, these secondary travel expenses are deductible. Keep track of the mileage if a car is used, as a mileage allowance is deductible.

If your total earned family income is under $10,000 for the year, you may be entitled to an earned income credit on your taxes.

Socializing expenses are only tax deductible if the entertainment is genuinely part of the job (for example, if it helps obtain new clients or increase business). Expenses for education or training required to maintain your job or for a license needed to perform that job are tax deductible.

Reading material associated with your job and any special equipment (such as a typewriter) are tax deductible. Office space in the home may be considered a tax-deductible item but this is tricky and should be checked into before making this claim.

Save proof of payment for a possible IRS challenge. Canceled checks or receipts will satisfy that requirement. Tax laws change frequently (nearly every year), so keep up with the new laws. For up-to-date information, call or write to your local IRS office.

19
Options and Possibilities

In recognition of women's need to have a family life and a job or career, new work options are evolving. Although they are not always readily available, business and government are gradually recognizing the benefits of offering nontraditional work arrangements to employees. Some of these options are:

1. *Flexible hours (flextime).* Employees have to work a set number of hours per week (usually forty), but the employee can determine those hours. They may have to be at work during peak business hours but have freedom in choosing other work hours. Under this system, morale and productivity are usually increased and absenteeism declines.

2. *Part-time work.* A worker is considered part-time if she works thirty-five hours a week or less. Usually fringe benefits are severely decreased with part-time employment, as is the opportunity for advancement. However, part-time work does afford you the time and opportunity to meet family obligations and may even leave you with some time for yourself.

3. *Job sharing.* In this arrangement, one job is shared by two individuals. Sometimes these two persons are husband and wife as in the mom and pop businesses of yesteryear. Benefits are prorated. Job-sharing programs are available in a large range of positions. Usually partners find each other; the job may or may not be split fifty-fifty. The hours and obligations are decided upon by the job sharers and may change with the workers' circumstances from week to week or month to month.

4. *Odd-hour jobs.* Work during the evening hours or at night might allow some women the opportunity to be employed. More and more businesses are open late in the evening, seven days a week, or even twenty-four hours a day.

5. *Working at home.* More and more businesses are allowing work to be done at home. Activities such as writing, making phone calls, reading, editing, and planning can be done at home. In addition, more home businesses are providing opportunities for satisfactory income, personal growth, and career fulfillment through self-employment. The major benefits of working at home are the familiar and secure working atmosphere, the freedom to set your own hours, the potential for privacy, and, of course, your availability to your children when they need you. The drawbacks of working at home are the interruptions due to other matters, the lack of co-workers, and the frustrating fact (at least at first) that you may not be taken seriously as a worker and provider by your family.

   If you do work at home, develop a working schedule for yourself and *stick to it*! Set aside a workplace in your home that is yours. Let friends and relatives know you are working at home; tell them your hours and ask them not to disturb you while you are working. Hire a sitter or day-care center to care for the kids while you are working. Preschedule breaks and lunches. You may need a telephone answering service or answering machine, or you may prefer to unplug the phone while you work.

6. *Forty-hour, four-day work week.* This option compresses the usual work week into four days, giving the worker three days off instead of two but requiring ten-hour work days.

7. *Day care at work.* Employer-sponsored child-care facilities close to the workplace were popular in the 1960s and 1970s, but the program has lost some of its appeal due to the lack of profit in the business. However, this may change as companies receive tax benefits when they provide child-care facilities for employees' children.

8. *All-day schools.* More and more schools are extending their programming to all day, especially in the kindergarten year. Before- and after-school programs in the form of latchkeys (see Chapter 9, "School Days," page 143) are becoming popular in some parts of the country. How-

ever, many of these programs are costly and place a financial burden on parents.

9. *Shared parenting.* The father participates as an equal partner in child-rearing and takes ultimate responsibility for certain activities rather than just "helping Mom." Although this does not mean splitting every task equally, it does mean cooperative parenting where each partner understands the time the children require and contributes his or her fair share in an equitable manner. A new, fully involved father's role is emerging and we will surely see more and more dads fulfilling (and expecting, and even demanding) extensive child-care responsibilities in the future.

10. *Maternity and paternity leaves.* Maternity and paternity leaves should be granted without fear of job loss. Although many businesses officially allow such leaves, prejudice and pressure are often felt by those who want to take off significant time when their child is born.

11. *Travel and transfers* as an option, not a requirement. Although some workers do not find travel difficult, others find it as a complete disruption to their family routines and life-styles. Required travel as well as required transfers for recognition or advancement should be held to a minimum in the business world. Uprooting one's family becomes more and more difficult when both parents work and family support systems have been established in a certain locale.

Check with your employer to see which of these options are available. Encourage him or her to offer as many of them as possible. Even if an option is not currently being offered on a regular basis (or at all), some employers are surprisingly willing to make special arrangements—especially if you do good work.

If you are looking for a job, you may wish to try to arrange one or more of these at the time you are hired. In any case, it doesn't hurt to ask if you do it properly; you have nothing to lose, and there is nothing wrong with being the first person at your workplace to make special working arrangements. You may also set a precedent for the benefit of other workers.

20

Further Information Sources

HEALTH CARE AND SAFETY

Arena, Joy M., and Miriam Bachar. *Child Safety Is No Accident.* New York: Hawthorne, 1978.

Boston Children's Medical Center. *Child Health Encyclopedia.* New York: Dell, 1978.

Boston Women's Health Collective. *Ourselves and Our Children.* New York: Random House, 1978.

Pantell, Robert H., James Fries, and Donald Vickery. *Taking Care of Your Child.* Reading, PA: Addison-Wesley, 1981.

Sehnert, Keith W. *The Family Doctor's Health Tips.* Minneapolis: Meadowbrook Press, 1981.

Shiller, Jack G. *Childhood Illness and Childhood Injury.* New York: Stein and Day, 1979.

Wynder, Ernest C., ed. *The Textbook of Health.* New York: Franklin Watts, 1981.

WORKING MOTHERS

Curtis, Jean. *A Guide for Working Mothers.* New York: Simon and Schuster, 1975.

Gabriel, Joyce, and Bettye Baldwin. *Having It All.* New York: Warner, 1980.

Greenleaf, Barbara Kaye. *Help, A Handbook for Working Mothers.* New York: Crowell, 1978.

Greiff, Barrie S., and Preston K. Munter. *Tradeoffs, Executive, Family and Organizational Life.* New York: Mentor, 1981.

Kuzma, Kay. *Working Mothers.* New York: Harper and Row, 1981.

Norris, Gloria, and Jo Ann Miller. *The Working Mother's Complete Handbook*. New York: Dutton, 1979.

Price, Jane. *How to Have a Child and Keep Your Job*. New York: Penguin, 1980.

CHILD CARE

Acus, Leah Kunkle. *Quarreling Kids*. Englewood Cliffs, NJ: Prentice-Hall, 1981.

Beebe, Brooke McKamy. *Best Bets for Babies*. New York: Dell, 1981.

Brazelton, T. Berry. *Infants and Mothers*. New York: Dell, 1981.

Cunningham, Cliff, and Patricia Sloper. *Helping Your Exceptional Baby*. New York: Pantheon, 1980.

Kelly, Marguerite, and Elia Parsons. *The Mother's Almanac*. New York: Doubleday, 1975.

Lansky, Vicki. *Best Practical Parenting Tips*. Minneapolis: Meadowbrook Press, 1980.

Pogrebin, Letty Cottin. *Growing Up Free*. New York: Bantam, 1980.

Sills, Barbara, and Jeanne Henry. *The Mother to Mother Baby Care Book*. New York: Avon, 1981.

Spock, Benjamin. *Baby and Child Care*, rev. ed. New York: Pocket Books, 1976.

Sullivan, S. Adams. *The Father's Almanac*. New York: Doubleday, 1980.

Touw, Kathleen. *Parent Tricks-of-the-Trade*. Washington: Acropolis, 1981.

Weinfeld, Nanci Rogoven. *Helpful Hints and Tricks for New Moms and Dads*. Chicago: Rand McNally, 1980.

Weiss, Joan Solomon. *Your Second Child*. New York: Summit, 1981.

While, Burton. *The First Three Years of Life*. New York: Avon, 1975.

CHILD-CARE CENTERS/BABYSITTING

Auerback, Stevanne. *Choosing Child Care*. New York: Dutton, 1981.

Barkin, Carol, and Elizabeth James. *The Complete Baby-sitter's Handbook*. New York: Simon and Schuster, 1980.

Benton, Barbara. *The Babysitter's Handbook*. New York: Morrow, 1981.

Endsley, Richard, and Marilyn Bradbard. *Quality Day Care*. Englewood Cliffs, NJ: Prentice-Hall, 1981.

Mitchell, Grace. *The Day Care Book*. New York: Fawcett, 1979.

Schick, Eleanor. *Home Alone*. New York: Dial, 1980.

TEENAGERS

Buntman, Peter H., and Eleanor M. Saris. *How to Live with Your Teenager*. Pasadena, CA: Birth Tree Press, 1979.

Feuerstein, Phillis, and Carol Roberts. *The Not-so-empty Nest*. Chicago: Follett, 1981.

McCoy, Kathy. *The Teenage Survival Guide*. New York: Simon and Schuster, 1981.

Rinzler, Carol Eisen. *Your Adolescent: An Owner's Manual*. New York: Atheneum, 1981.

Schowalter, John E., and Walter R. Anyan. *The Family Handbook of Adolescence*. New York: Knopf, 1981.

SINGLE PARENTING/DIVORCE

Atkin, Edith, and Estelle Rubin. *Part-time Fathers*. New York: Signet, 1976.

Galper, Miriam. *Joint Custody and Co-parenting*. Philadelphia: Running Press, 1980.

Gatley, Richard, and David Koulack. *Single Father's Handbook*. New York: Anchor, 1979.

Hope, Karol, and Nancy Young, eds. *Momma, the Sourcebook for Single Mothers*. New York: Plume, 1976.

Knight, Bryan M. *Enjoying Single Parenthood*. New York: Van Nostrand Reinhold, 1980.

Silver, Gerald, and Myrna Silver. *Weekend Fathers*. New York: Harper and Row, 1981.

Vigenveno, H. S., and Ann Claire. *Divorce and the Children*. Glendale, CA: Regal Books, 1979.

Wallerstein, Judith S., and Joan Berlin Kelly. *Surviving the Breakup.* New York: Basic Books, 1980.

Weiss, Robert S. *Going It Alone.* New York, Basic Books: 1979.

ORGANIZATION

Aslett, Don. *Is There Life after Housework?* Cincinnati: Writer's Digest, 1981.

Heloise. *Hints from Heloise.* New York: Avon, 1980.

Hughes, Martha Ellen. *The* Woman's Day *Book of Household Hints.* New York: Morrow, 1978.

Pinkham, Mary Ellen. *Mary Ellen's Best of Helpful Hints, Book II.* New York: Warner, 1981.

Winston, Stephanie. *Getting Organized.* New York: Warner, 1979.

GENERAL READING

Badinter, Elisabeth. *Mother Love.* New York: Macmillan, 1980.

Friedan, Betty. *The Second Stage.* New York: Summit, 1981.

USEFUL NUMBERS AND NOTES

_____

_____

_____

_____

_____

_____

_____

_____

_____

_____

_____

USEFUL NUMBERS AND NOTES

_____

_____

_____

_____

_____

_____

_____

_____

_____

_____

_____

USEFUL NUMBERS AND NOTES

_____

_____

_____

_____

_____

_____

_____

_____

_____

_____

_____

_____

USEFUL NUMBERS AND NOTES

_____

_____

_____

_____

_____

_____

_____

_____

_____

_____

_____

ABOUT THE AUTHOR

Gloria Gilbert Mayer is a very active working mother. She is a registered nurse with a doctorate in education from Columbia University; a health care and hospital consultant (which requires her to travel throughout the United States and Canada); co-owner of a restaurant; and a writer, lecturer, and teacher.

Gloria lives with her husband, Tom (a physician and writer), her daughter, Kimmel, and her son, Jeffrey, in Minnetonka, Minnesota, near Minneapolis.

Gloria has published more than forty professional articles and a textbook on nursing (Springer, 1982), and has received many honors in nursing. She lectures and teaches widely on dual-career families, working women and working mothers, and a variety of nursing and health-care issues.